HEART THROBS FROM THE BENCH

HEART THROBS FROM
THE BENCH

By

MINTER L. WILSON
*Former Judge of the Seventeenth
Judicial Circuit of West Virginia*

Author
of
"Patriot Truth"

The Christopher Publishing House
Boston, U. S. A.

DEDICATION

This book has been made possible by the loyalty and fidelity of the good people of the great and beautiful Mountain State of West Virginia. It is therefore affectionately dedicated to them, with the hope that I may continue to deserve their confidence, respect and goodwill.

CONTENTS

PART I
SERVICE

PART IV

WAR

PART V

CHILDREN

CONTENTS

9

PART VI

THE DEVELOPMENT OF LAW AND ITS IMPORTANCE

PART VII

THE SECURITY OF AMERICA

FOREWORD

Every statement in this book was made by me from the Bench while sitting as Judge of the 17th Judicial Circuit of West Virginia, from January 1, 1937, to January 1, 1945, a period in which the world was engulfed in turmoil and the nations of the earth were bewildered, confused and harassed by a terrific world storm. There is back of each thought a situation and an occasion. This book is not the result of cold logic in solving legal problems, but of warm and fervent thought where human problems are involved. It is filled with sparks from the judicial anvil, and is the by-product of decisions and reactions where human hearts, the public welfare and the security of America are involved.

The thoughts expressed in this book, it seems to me, are most appropriate for the reading public of America at this time, since a new world crisis has appeared on the horizon.

Apparently there is no book of this nature available in America. This book is, therefore, published to fill a considerable need and for the benefit of the Bench, the Bar and the American public.

Minter L. Wilson

Morgantown, West Virginia
November 1, 1949.

PART I
SERVICE

ledge is immediately connected with all the highest interests of the people of this community.

It is my desire that you represent your clients well. You all have your own methods of effectiveness. Your clients deserve the best that is in you. The more effective you are for your clients, the more respect you will have from the judge of this court. If you should accidentally overstep the bounds of propriety in your enthusiasm for your clients, you will be reminded of that fact.

The office of sheriff was established by the Constitution of West Virginia. The office of sheriff is a most ancient one, dating back to the time of Alfred, King of England. He is not a judicial officer. The sheriff's deputies, constables, state police, and municipal officers are not judicial officers. They all act in an administrative capacity in performing their duties, and not as judges of the evidence or facts surrounding the commission of a crime. None of the officers I have mentioned has any right to express his opinion as to who was the cause of an accident. It is his duty to gather facts, and to give these facts to the proper tribunal when called upon.

Suppose the driver of an automobile has killed a pedestrian, let us say a child. No enforcement officer has a right to pass on the innocence or guilt of the driver. No officer has a right to exonerate the driver.

It is the province of a judicial officer or body to pass
on that. It is the enforcement officer's duty to take
offenders into custody, and deliver them to a place
of safe keeping. His duties are then over, unless
called upon to testify. A judicial officer's duty begins where the enforcement officer's duty ends. No
person who has caused the death of a human being,
even though not intentional, should be released, except by a judicial officer or tribunal, after a proper
hearing.

A word to the public. Under the law the judge
has no right to discuss cases before him, or which may
come before him, with individuals. A judge's mind
must be kept free from all outside influences. I request
that no individual embarrass me or himself by attempt-
ing to discuss any case with me. It will be my policy to
carry on the work of this court in the open. This
court is for all the people. All my decisions will be
based on the law and the evidence brought before
the court in the proper manner. I will not tolerate
outside influences, political or otherwise.

In my speech accepting the nomination for the
judgeship, I said: "I have learned to love the people
of this county. They have been very kind to me.
If elected to this high honor, I will be their servant."
That statement stands.

As judge of this court, I will ask for Divine Guidance as I have been accustomed to do as a private citizen. May God bless all the people of this county, and bring to all of us a happier and fuller life during the coming years.

CHAPTER TWO

IMPORTANCE OF THE GRAND JURY

Gentlemen of the Grand Jury:

Your appearance here today in this capacity brings to you the highest honor that can come to a private citizen in this great county. You have been chosen from among a population of more than fifty thousand people. You would not be here today, if you were not men of good moral character; or if you had ever been convicted of a felony, or any scandalous offense. You would not be here today in this service, if you were not outstanding citizens.

A few days ago on the occasion of my induction into office as judge of this court, I made a statement from the bench to the people of the county. Among other things, I said: "As Judge of this court I am your servant. This court is master of us all. It stands here an institution which we have inherited. It embodies the best that all the generations down through the ages have produced. It is made up of all the tenderness, the love, the charity, the firmness, the noble sacrifices, the intelligence and the justice of the past. The Old Testament is one of its cornerstones, but it is infused with the benign temper of the New Testament. It is so tender and kindly in its nature that it shelters the frailest right of the weakest in this county; and yet it is so powerful and strong that it checks and stays the assault of the mightiest. We are perpetuating this institution we call the Court, and which we have inherited, because we cannot have happiness, peace, and prosperity without it."

I repeat that statement to you gentlemen today in the belief that it will give you a clearer understanding of your service. You are an instrument of this court, just as much so as the judge. You are servants of the people. How true were the words of the Master when He said, "He that is greatest among you shall be servant of all."

The grand jury is of very ancient origin in the history of England. At the time of the origin of the grand jury, there were struggles between the powers of the King and the rights of the people. Before the origin of the grand jury, the people of England were many times persecuted in the name of the Crown. Since the existence of this institution we call the grand jury, it has stood as a barrier against any persecution of the people of England in the name of the King. That was the reason for its existence. Thus, we see the original purpose of the grand jury was for the protection of the people. Gentlemen, that is its purpose today. Since the settlement of this country, the grand jury has always protected the people against any persecution on the part of the government. The grand jury is not only the foundation, it is the bulwark of our liberties.

So, gentlemen, we see that while it is the incidental duty of the grand jury to bring to trial persons accused of offenses upon just grounds, the primary purpose of the grand jury is to protect the citizens of this county against unfounded accusations, whether they come from officials of the government, or are prompted by partisan passion or private enmity.

You represent both the government and the people. Both the government and the people are most certainly concerned that all crimes should receive the punishment prescribed by law; but on the other hand both the government and the people should be equally concerned that innocence should, after careful investigation, be securely protected.

Both the State of West Virginia and the Federal Government, realizing the importance of the grand jury, have put it out of the reach of any man or any set of men, and placed its continued existence entirely with the people.

The Constitution of West Virginia has placed the grand jury beyond the possibility of legislative abrogation in its "Bill of Rights" providing that: "No person shall be held to answer for treason, felony or other crime, not cognizable by a justice, unless on presentment or indictment of a grand jury."

In the Federal jurisprudence the grand jury has been placed beyond the possibility of Congressional abrogation by the Fifth Amendment to the Constitution of the United States, which provides that: "No person shall be held to answer for a capital or otherwise infamous crime, unless on a presentment or indictment of a grand jury . . ."

I desire to call to your attention the instructions of Moses to his people, in the sixteenth and seventeenth verses of the first chapter of Deuteronomy. Moses there said: "And I charged your judges at that time, saying, hear the causes between your brethren, and judge righteously between every man and his brother and the stranger that is with him.

"Ye shall not respect persons in judgment; but ye shall hear the small as well as the great; ye shall not be afraid of the face of man; for the judgment is God's and the cause that is too hard for you, bring it unto me and I will hear it."

The Supreme Court of Appeals of West Virginia has defined the grand jury to be a judicial tribunal. You are the sole judges of the evidence that comes before you. I commend those instructions of Moses to you; and I particularly emphasize the instruction not to respect persons, and to hear the small as well as the great.

Those instructions of Moses to his judges have the same general tone as the oath you have just taken. One limitation of your oath is that you shall present no person through malice, hatred or ill will; another limitation of your oath is that you shall not leave any person unpresented through fear, favor, partiality or affection.

CHAPTER THREE

ADDRESS TO NEW CITIZENS

Since 1932 a proposal has been in the platform of the National Education Association which reads as follows:

"Provisions should be made to receive all persons into citizenship with suitable ceremony."

In 1940 Congress passed a joint resolution which reads as follows:

"Either at the time of the rendition of the decree of naturalization, or at such other time as the Judge may fix, the Judge or someone else designated by him shall address the newly naturalized citizens upon the form and genius of our government, and the privileges and responsibilities of citizenship."

It is my purpose today to comply with the above resolution of Congress and to dignify and emphasize the significance of citizenship.

I congratulate you on becoming citizens of the United States. I noticed that some of you took this oath of allegiance with tears of gratitude. Many of you have breathed the foul air of oppression in a foreign country. You have just joined the great family of citizens who are enjoying the cherished principles of freedom.

You have just pledged yourselves to a great ideal. I know that you intend to do your part to sustain and uphold that ideal. You are becoming a part of this nation, just as the nation becomes a part of you. You have just been granted a privilege. You have been offered an opportunity. You have just received the most cherished heritage in the gift of humanity

Americans everywhere have implicit faith in the American way of life. In these dark hours of our civilization when the loyalty of all is essential to victory, I desire to emphasize at this time and from this bench the fact that all creeds and all races have made America. At this time I desire to point out, not only for the benefit and encouragement of you new citizens, but for the benefit of all citizens, some contributions that have been made to the American way of life by some foreign born Americans.

Jacob Riis was born in Denmark. President Theodore Roosevelt once characterized him as the most useful American of his day and the nearest to the ideal of an American citizen.

James J. Hill was a native of Canada. He was the "Empire Builder." He made thousands of men and women happier because of his clear vision and faith in the future of the great Northwest.

Michael Pupin was born in Yugoslavia. He was the shepherd boy who became one of America's greatest teachers and scientists. Among his inventions is the "tuning in" mechanism that controls every radio.

Samuel Gompers, the great labor leader, was born in England. It was through his untiring efforts that the dignity and worth of labor became recognized.

Father Edward Flanagan came to this country from Ireland. He has done more than anyone else in the fight against juvenile delinquency, with the philosophy: "There is no such thing as a bad boy." He is recognized all over America as an inspirational leader working in behalf of American youth.

Joseph Pulitzer came here from Hungary. He founded the famous newspaper called The New York World. He gave one million dollars to Columbia University for the first school of journalism in America. He is the man who raised funds to bring the Bartholdi Statue of Liberty from France to America and place it at the entrance to New York Harbor.

Carl Schurz, who came to this country from Germany, was the loyal friend of Abraham Lincoln and one of his first supporters for the Presidency. He loved and understood America. America's finest concept of patriotism may be found in the immortal words of Carl Schurz, which were:

"My country, right or wrong; if right, to be kept right, if wrong, to be set right."

Alexander Bell was born in Scotland, but as an American he gave to the world one of the greatest inventions of all times, the telephone.

Angelo Patri was an immigrant from Italy. He became a great teacher. He placed emphasis upon the child and helped the parent to better understand the child. Out of the teaching of Angelo Patri, an immigrant from Italy, grew the first Parent-Teacher Association in America. This immigrant placed in America a historic milestone in the educational field.

Louis Adamic, who is one of our famous foreign born Americans, was born in Slovenia. He once said:

"Most of our thirty-eight million immigrants of the last century were escaping from oppression of some kind, either political or economic. To them, as to the Pilgrims, America was a refuge, a chance for a better life."

Irving Berlin came here from Russia. He recently said:

"I was so grateful and thankful to be an American citizen, I just had to do something to express that feeling, and, being a song writer, I wanted to write a song about it. Of the many songs I have written in the past thirty years, I think 'God Bless America' is nearest my heart."

The native land of William Knudsen is Denmark. You all know him by reputation. He recently said:

"An immigrant is just another name for pioneer. We all came here to find independence and self-expression as much as wealth. America treats its people decently, protects their constitutional guarantees, gives them a chance to make a living and educate their children. All Americans, whether they are native or foreign born, will treat America decently in return."

Madame Schumann-Heink, who thrilled America for more than a quarter of a century with her beautiful voice, came here from Germany with her six small children. She once said:

"Blessed Land, America, gave us everything . . . opportunities, benefits, and, above all, Freedom of heart, mind and soul . . . she accepted us and trusted us to the fullest extent when we came as strangers to this land, and even in these troubled times . . . surely, my sons, surely this is a land worth fighting for."

This statement was made during the First World War. It was made to her sons, and she sent six sons to fight for America and against the people of her native land.

I have given you only a few examples of those who brought their gifts to America. Throughout our history some immigrants have reached and achieved greatness in various fields of activity. But these few who have achieved greatness, along with the native born Americans who achieved greatness, could never have made America great. It is the countless thousands from the great common people, who do their duty from day to day and are never noticed except by their neighbors, who have contributed most toward making America what it is today. I think it is fitting at this time, not only to impress upon you new citizens, but to impress upon every citizen, the worth and importance of the ordinary man.

Some of the rights of every American citizen, including all those who are naturalized, are:

1. The right to Constitutional Government.
2. Freedom of Religion.
3. Freedom of Speech and of the Press.
4. Freedom of Peaceable Assembly.
5. The right to Petition.
6. The right of every citizen to be secure in his "Person, house, papers and effects."
7. Protection against being deprived of life, liberty or property without due process of law.
8. The right when accused of crime, to have the charges first considered by a Grand Jury.
9. The right to a trial by a Jury, selected fairly and properly.
10. Protection in the rights of citizenship regardless of race, color, religion, economic conditions or political affiliations.

Along with all these rights go your responsibilities. You have just taken an oath to support and defend the Constitution and laws of the United States of America against all enemies, foreign and domestic. You have just become sovereign citizens. You now have upon your shoulders the preservation of the Freedom of America for which others have paid so dearly.

American citizenship is a glorious possession representing the dreams and the struggles of men for centuries. Our Bill of Rights is a charter of human liberty, but it was obtained at a high price. It was achieved through struggles, suffering and sacrifice. Men from dark dungeons, corpses swinging from gallows, human torches lit by the flame of intolerance, victims of the Inquisition, patriots who suffered and died in the Revolutionary War, in the First World War, in the Second World War and on other battlefields of freedom have played their part in securing and preserving this charter of human liberty.

You have just come into a precious heritage. Preserve it well, and tonight get down on your knees and thank God for this blessing.

CHAPTER FOUR

JURY SERVICE

Gentlemen of the Jury:

Your call to jury service is not a matter of chance. When you will be called to jury service is a matter of chance, but the fact you are called is one of deliberate selection. Jury service is a selected service. You would not be here today, if the jury commissioners had not come to the conclusion that you were of sound judgment and of good moral character.

America has only one aristocracy. That is the aristocracy of service. You belong to that aristocracy.

American citizenship means something. The fact you are an American citizen throws around you many safeguards. I have thanked God many times that fate made me a citizen of this greatest of all nations. You and I have inherited the best that every Christian generation has produced. This is a democracy. This is a country where the people rule themselves. This is not a totalitarian nation. In this country your life, your liberty, or your property cannot be taken away from you, unless and until twelve of your neighbors say it should be taken away.

American citizenship carries with it many obligations. One of those obligations is jury service. I have learned from my experience on this bench that there are some citizens, who have been placed in that class of aristocracy to which I have just referred, who do not appreciate what it means to them to be an American citizen, and who do not realize their obligations of American citizenship.

It is just as important for every citizen to serve his country faithfully, in peace time, as it is for him to fight for his country, courageously, in time of war.

PART II

PATRIOTISM

PART II

PATRIOTISM

CHAPTER FIVE

THE MAKING OF THE AMERICAN FLAG— (HUMANITY'S IMMORTAL CREATION)

God alone created the rose. But God and humanity worked together for 1777 years to create the American Flag.

In the 25th Chapter of Leviticus, we hear God speaking to Moses on Mount Sinai, saying, "Proclaim liberty throughout all the land unto all the inhabitants thereof." That command has come down through the ages, and was recorded as an inscription on the Liberty Bell in Philadelphia long before the Declaration of Independence. The American Flag is humanity's noble and glorious answer to that divine command. The American Flag had its conception at the time of the birth of Christ. Its history is parallel with the history of Christianity. It springs from new concepts of human relationships which came from the teachings, not of the high and mighty of the earth, but of the greatest humanitarian of the ages,—the lowly Nazarene. The American Flag is immortal because it springs from eternal truth.

The spirit of liberty nestled in the hearts of men before the birth of our Saviour, but up to the time of that event nothing had happened in the world to give definite and continuous expression to that feeling in the hearts of men. Christianity not only gave that necessary expression, but it also fed and nourished that God given spirit in men which is the foundation of liberty.

Christianity was a message to the individual. It renewed his mind; it transformed him; it proclaimed the worth of his personality; it substituted him for the group. For the first time in the history of the world the individual became important. This new conception of the individual started liberty on its onward and upward march, and also started the prenatal history of the American Flag. Its history is parallel with the history of liberty. For 1777 years the American Flag existed in its prenatal form.

The Cathedral of Notre Dame in Paris was six centuries in building. Its pillars are Roman; its pointed arches are Gothic; it has the stained windows of the 13th century, and the painted windows of modern times. That cathedral is a history of science and art during those six centuries. It is a product of human society. May we not say the same of the American

Flag? Is it not a product of human society? May we not say that every wave of time has added its deposit; every generation has made its contribution?

In the Boston Public Library there is a remarkable painting by the great American artist, John Singer Sargent, entitled, "The Triumph of Religion". This painting was in the process of making for more than twenty-five years. To merely narrate the history of the cloth of the American Flag and stop there would be like narrating the different stages through which the great artist has gone in producing a work of genius, without pointing out the fundamental truths which made that painting possible.

Time passes, and we see the barbarians of the North sweeping down over Rome and conquering it. It looks as if the world will be sunk in the darkness of ignorance, but the light of Christianity shines, and we see Clovis, King of the Franks, accepting Christianity, and we see the barbarians bowing before the cross.

Now the Mohammedans pour across the Mediterranean and ravage the Christian nations, and at the battle of Tours we see Charles Martel routing them and driving them back. Again the world is saved for liberty, and for the American Flag.

History expands, and crosses the English Channel into what is now England. The future character of that unborn Flag was influenced at Runnymede when the Barons wrested Magna Charta from King John, one clause of which reads, "We will sell to no man, we will not deny or delay to any man right or justice."

History now crosses into the mountains of Scotland. There Sir William Wallace nobly supports the liberty of Scotland, and today the name of William Wallace has a romantic charm as a hero of the liberty of his country, and the name of Scotland has become synonymous with that of liberty.

The center of interest has shifted to the mountainous and romantic country of Switzerland. The Swiss have defeated the Austrians and asserted their independence of the House of Austria, and the future cast of that Flag was being made. But the Austrians again attack them, and Arnold of Winkelried exclaimed, "Make way for liberty." He made way for liberty and died, and that liberty which he made way for was existing when more than one thousand Englishmen fled to Switzerland during the fearful reign of Mary. Of the influence which the liberty of Switzerland had on the world, Rufus Choate says, "I ascribe to that five years in Geneva an influence which has changed the history of the world. I seem to myself to trace to it, as an influence on the English race, a new theology; another tone of character; the opening of another era of time and of liberty. I seem to myself to trace to it the great Civil War of England; the Republican Constitution framed in the cabin of the Mayflower; the divinity of Jonathan Edwards; the battle of Bunker Hill; the independence of America." That Flag was being molded then in Switzerland.

That Flag was being fashioned when William, Prince of Orange, appeared on the scene as the defender of liberty against the tyranny of Philip the Second of Spain; when he said, "What greater glory can there be than to maintain the liberty of a man's country, and to die rather than to be enslaved." That Flag took shape and form in Holland under the benign and wholesome influence of that liberty which William, Prince of Orange, preserved; for the pilgrims had lived in Holland for eleven years where they had enjoyed and studied its free democratic institutions, before they set out for America. Broadhead, in his History of New York, says that to no nation in the world is the United States more indebted than to the United Provinces of Holland for the idea of the confederation of sovereign states, and for noble principles of constitutional freedom. Thus we see the patriots of the Old World made the Stars and Stripes a possibility. It was the task of the New World to make the Flag a reality.

"The Mayflower rides serenely on yonder bay,
Mute Convoy of immortal souls,
Proudly heaving with majestic sway
As each wave toward the shore of freedom rolls."

The flag is still in its prenatal stage but it continues to evolve. The pilgrims signed their constitution in the cabin of the Mayflower November 11, 1620, the first written constitution in the history of the world. This constitution Lincoln calls the foundation of the Republic. This constitution contained new concepts of human relationships. It did not set forth the doctrine of the divine right of kings and dictators; it set forth the doctrine of the divine rights of the people.

It was not long after the foundation of the Republic was laid, before a tyrannical king thrust his iron hand into the affairs of the American people. But God had raised up great leaders. Washington, Franklin, Jefferson, Patrick Henry and many other patriots appeared on the stage. The guns are heard at Lexington and Bunker Hill. The Declaration of Independence is announced to the world.

The Declaration of Independence, July 4, 1776, is especially important, because it was the final act which made our Flag possible. A Flag which was conceived in liberty and went through its long prenatal period in oppression is about to be born in struggle. A nation as Lincoln refers to it, is conceived in liberty and dedicated to the proposition that all men are created equal. The Declaration of Independence propounded the doctrine that all men are endowed by their Creator with certain inalienable rights, that among these are life, liberty and the pursuit of happiness. That was a brave doctrine in a world filled with kings. The Declaration of Independence was a divine instrument of human liberty. Without it our Flag would never have been born.

Thus far in the history of liberty, the cloth of our Flag had not come into existence. Our Flag is now about to be born. At the time of the Declaration of Independence, the "Union Flag" existed, having been displayed in Cambridge, Massachusetts, by Washington for the first time January 1, 1776. This flag had thirteen stripes and the Union Jack, as we still showed our loyalty to England, and were only fighting for our rights before the Declaration of Independence. June 14, 1777, the Continental Congress adopted a resolution that our Flag be thirteen stripes, and that the Union Jack be replaced by thirteen stars. Tradition says that Betsy Ross actually designed and made the first American Flag in June, 1777.

We see now that our Flag did not suddenly spring into existence. The making of our Flag has been the work of centuries.

The Declaration of Independence and the Revolutionary War marked the birth of a new nation. But the mere birth of a nation does not assure its future, or its liberty. That new nation consisted of thirteen weak states loosely bound together. The future of that new

nation was assured when our pioneer forefathers stood
on the edge of civilization, with a vision, and fashioned
a Constitution broad enough to extend to the Pacific,
and elastic enough to encompass one economic unit.
The liberty of that new nation was assured when the
Bill of Rights was made a part of that Constitution.
The Constitution of the United States stands today as
the supreme law of the land, and the faithful servant
of that Flag which waves supreme over all.

Soon after the adoption of the Constitution of the
United States, we see liberty on its onward and upward
march in the little island of Haiti. The population of
Haiti was made up of whites, mulattoes and unmixed
negroes. One-half million negroes had been trans-
planted to the island from Africa and sold as slaves, to
work there on the rich sugar plantation.

The island of Haiti was controlled by the Spaniards,
the French, the English, and mulattoes. All negroes
were slaves.

At this time there lived on the island of Haiti an unmixed negro whose father had been brought from
Africa. He was uneducated, but he proved to be an in-
spired man. He was a military genius and a statesman.
His name was Toussaint L'Ouverture. He manufac-
tured an army out of the slaves of Haiti; out of men
who were ignorant and unable to understand each
other's dialect. He fought for the liberty of his people.

He defeated the proud Spaniard, and sent him home conquered. He put the French, who at that time under Napoleon had conquered most of Europe, under his control. He drove the English to the island of Jamaica. He was known as the Black Napoleon; but Napoleon made slaves, while Toussaint L'Ouverture freed them. Napoleon fought for power, while Toussaint L'Ouverture fought for liberty.

At this time Napoleon determined again to make slaves out of the negroes of Haiti. He sent sixty thousand of his best troops to the island for this purpose. The blacks, led by Toussaint L'Ouverture, defeated them in the field. The French then resorted to strategy and propaganda. They promised the negroes their liberty and freedom. Toussaint L'Ouverture and his followers laid down their arms. The French betrayed them. Toussaint L'Ouverture was put on a boat and taken to France. As he dropped below the horizon and could no longer see Haiti, he turned to his betrayers and said: "You think you have rooted up the tree of liberty; I have planted the tree so deep that all France can never root it up."

Toussaint L'Ouverture was delivered to Napoleon, who starved him to death in a dungeon. His followers then rushed to arms to fight again for their liberty. The fifty thousand graves of Napoleon's best soldiers in Haiti speak eloquently as to how well the tree of liberty was planted. Napoleon failed to root it up, and he exclaimed to that little remnant of his army who returned to France: "I gave you an army; you bring me back ashes."

Toussaint L'Ouverture, a martyr for the liberty of his people, was the forerunner of the Great Emancipator.

Abraham Lincoln added luster to the stars in our Flag, when he issued his Proclamation of Emancipation on January 1, 1863. In striking slavery down in this country, Lincoln became the greatest benefactor of the human race, for as James Russell Lowell says, "Only that good lasts which we can taste with all doors open and which serves all men. When we have a part of our population in bondage, we destroy that spirit which prizes liberty, and plant the seeds of despotism at our own doors."

It took God and humanity 1777 years to produce that Flag of thirteen stars. In 166 years there have been added thirty-five new stars.

In 1776 there streamed through the veins of the youth of this country that patriotic blood which bade them nobly die, rather than see their country ravaged by an inexorable tyrant. An example of that patriotism is evidenced by the last utterance of Nathan Hale, —"I only regret that I have but one life to lose for my country."

In 1918 there streamed through the veins of the youth of this country that warmer patriotic blood, which bade them nobly die, not only rather than allow the Stars and Stripes trespassed upon, but also rather than see the flags of liberty-loving nations trampled upon by those who were impelled by the desire of greed and conquest. An example of that warmer patriotic blood is the picture of two million American youths crossing an ocean three thousand miles wide, filled with dangerous submarines; landing in a strange country; hurling the Kaiser's best troops back from the Marne; and driving the Kaiser's forces of tyranny back through the forests of the Argonne.

The youth of America gave new luster to the stars in our Flag in that greatest of all crusades on the battlefields of France, where they upheld the honor and the traditions of America. Let us take a glimpse at that crusade.

It is now the evening of the 9th of July, 1917. Come aboard the Baltic Steamship in New York Harbor. Let's go up on deck, for I hear the men yelling, "She's pulling out." See the men climbing the mast; hear the farewell songs; look at the ships swarming around us, puffing and whistling, like a great holiday throng. The countless lights of New York twinkle everywhere back of us. The sun has left us with reluctance, for yonder to the West she sends back her golden reflection which hangs there in the western sky above America like a great painting; so that the last object our eyes fall upon, after we can no longer see America, will be a symbol of America's splendor and glory.

There is the Statue of Liberty enlightening the world, rising on the bosom of a wave, holding aloft the torch which sheds its rays far into the sea. That statue is a treaty of friendship between America and France,—a treaty signed by all hearts of both nations. How fitting that it was made in France by a French sculptor, and that it should now stand here as a gift from France, lighting our way to the country from which it came. It knows our errand. It knows that we are impelled by the same emotions as those who gave to it its existence. It bids us farewell.

I now perceive the expanse of the ocean. I hear the solemn murmur of the waves as they break against the sides of the ship. The golden reflection of the descending sun has softened into purple tints, giving us a symbol of our country's majesty and power. The twilight's purple majesty now deepens into blue. The lights of New York are disappearing. We are dropping below the horizon into a dangerous sea infested with German submarines.

We are now in the Irish Sea. It has been eight days since we said farewell to the Statue of Liberty and the fair land of America. We have no convoy; we are left to the mercy of the German submarines. According to a wireless received yesterday, the Germans are now reaping their largest submarine harvest, and they are the most active in this zone. A convoy was due to meet us two days ago. We are now in the most dangerous part of the "danger zone". The order on the ship is "silence". The soldiers are permitted to spend the night on the deck of the ship. There is nothing to see except the indistinct expanse of the ocean and the darkness hovering down close upon us. There is nothing to hear except the occasional groan of an American soldier, and the melancholy murmuring and moaning of the waves, as if complaining at the progress of the ship, as they break against its sides. As the ship turns on its zig-zagging course, this moaning breaks into a wailing, as if to add a stronger protest against the ship's progress. But a new day will soon be here. The soldiers on the deck are beginning to stir. The darkness to the East yonder is breaking into banks and streaming lines of color. Men are rising and looking into the distance. See how intently they turn their eyes to the East. The morning sun breaks through the mist, and the waves are illumined by its splendor.

A mysterious object floats in the distance on one of these illumined waves. It is too far in the distance for us to distinguish it as any definite object. Now it disappears. There it is again. It comes nearer and nearer.

The form of something is silhouetted in the mist above
that mysterious object. It resembles the outline of a
flag. But what flag? It approaches rapidly. It comes
nearer and nearer. It is a submarine destroyer that
plows so boldly through the waves, and that silhouetted object that seemed to come through the gates of
Heaven with the morning has transformed itself, and
there before our eyes, in the jewelled mist of the morning, floats the Stars and Stripes. Hear the spontaneous
cheers, even though the order is "silence".

Why the cheers? Because our souls are at this time
in harmony with the great truths which that Flag
carries within its folds. Do we see only the cloth of
that Flag? No. Through the eyes that have been made
clear, we see more than that. My memory connecting
the past with the present, and my imagination, stimu-
lated by the sight of the Stars and Stripes as it waves
there like a fringe of the garment of God, bring to the
folds of that Flag the happy homes of West Virginia,
sitting like jewels between its majestic mountains,
nestled among its hills and valleys, and grouped into
beautiful cities along its winding rivers.

The shades of evening come down quietly on those
happy homes. The sheep come from their refuge
under the shade of the great oaks, and wend their way
toward the little streams. Men come from the mines,
from the factories, from the shops, from the fields,

from the offices, from everywhere to take refuge with
their families within the walls of their happy homes,
homes as secure and sacred, under the law, as the
King's palace in England, or the White House in
Washington. There the fathers are masters of their
destinies. Their persons are inviolate. They can law-
fully repel attacks upon those homes with the greatest
force. There the fathers retire with their families
within the four walls of their castles, and are free from
the baffles of society. There the essential personal
rights are beyond the jurisdiction of the community.
There are certain fireside rights which their forefathers did not delegate to the government. There the
fathers sit before their hearthstones with their minds
free, and they can thus devise as they think best for
their families; their consciences are free, and thus they
can worship their God as they please.

The devoted wives sit there, happy in the thought of
their families, their husbands' companions, their equals,
sharing in their joys and triumphs, and consoling them
in their adversities and their sorrows.

I hear the children's childish glee; see them in their
games and in their intellectual pursuits, until sleep demands its supremacy, and they kiss their fathers and
mothers "good night".

We had seen the heart of our Flag; the citadel of
this government.

In this war today for the survival of civilization, millions, not only in America, but throughout the world, are seeing more than the cloth of the American Flag.

The making of the American Flag is not completed. It continues to grow and develop and mature. The soldiers of today are the makers of the Flag. They are making the Flag in many far flung areas of the earth,— in Alaska, the Aleutian Islands, Australia, China, India, Burma, New Guinea, the Solomons, Panama, South America, Iceland, Greenland, Ireland, England, Africa, Sicily and over, in, and under the water and on the islands of the Atlantic and the Pacific Oceans, and the Mediterranean Sea.

The brave soldiers who so gallantly defended Wake Island, Bataan Peninsula and Corregidor added a luster to the stars in our Flag that will never be sullied. The bold and daring American sailors and aviators who so valiantly and successfully defended Australia in the Coral Sea, and our line of defense in the Midway Island area, and annihilated the Japs in the Bismarck Sea, added a new glory to Old Glory.

Those fearless, pioneer Americans, led by "Jimmie" Doolittle, who flew the B-25 bombers on their destructive sweep over Japan, glorified that Flag in the hearts of a freedom loving people.

Our land, air and sea forces, including tough marines

and trained parachute troops who for the first time in this war cooperated in an offensive action, showed us the soul of America and the heart of our Flag when they slugged the Japs into insensibility and hurled them from Guadalcanal. They were heroic makers of the Flag.

Our dauntless American forces who swept across the sands of Northern Africa and the mud of Tunisia and with the cooperation of the French and the British, decisively defeated the vaunted Africa Korps of Marshal Rommel, were dramatic makers of the Flag.

The daring and unterrified American soldiers who landed on the cold, bleak, desolate, wild, dreary and fog-bound, but strategic Island of Attu, utterly destroyed and exterminated the Japanese forces there and captured that island, are mighty makers of the Flag.

Those adventurous and stout-hearted American forces who crossed the Mediterranean from Africa, and cooperating with the Canadians and the English invaded Sicily and punctured the underbelly of the so-called Fortress of Europe, are historic makers of the Flag.

Every lover of liberty down through history has been a maker of the Flag. It is the result of the progress of the ages. It represents the best that every Christian generation has produced. We are all makers of the Flag. It is a result of our dreams and our toil; our aspirations and our hopes; our faith and our courage; our strength and our weakness. It is a symbol of America.

That Flag is made with the blood and the sweat and the tears of generations that had resisted tyrants for the right to live. It comes from the triumphs of liberty in dark places. It is made of all the tenderness, the love, the purity, the faith, the firmness, the noble sacrifices, the intelligence, the courage, and the justice of the past. In the Old Testament we find the command for its existence; but we find its substance in the New Testament.

That Flag knows no creeds, no classes, no organizations. It is not narrow; it is not bigoted; it is not intolerant. That Flag not only demands the same loyalty from all, but also guarantees the same opportunity to all who live beneath its folds.

That Flag stands for the sanctity of the home; the sublime sentiments of the family; and the sacredness of the Christian religion. That Flag symbolizes our priceless heritage of liberty.

That Flag is the bulwark of democracy; it is the safeguard of the Christian Cross. That Flag, which was made possible by the patriots of the Old World, returns to them. It shines in the dark places of Europe and Asia; it warms the hearts of those who sit in bondage. Some day its warmth will melt away tyranny and dictatorships, and that Flag will be waving for democracy and the Christian Cross when Hitler and Mussolini and Tojo and all their satellites are gone and forgotten.

It is an exalted privilege and a precious opportunity to fight for that Flag; to fight for the freedom of religion, free speech, a free press, the right to assemble, the right to be secure in your person and in your own home, the right to the judgment of a Grand Jury before you can be prosecuted for a crime, the right to a public and impartial jury trial, the right to equality of opportunity. Yes, it is an exalted privilege to fight for all of those rights and to fight for those inalienable rights of life, liberty and the pursuit of happiness mentioned in the Declaration of Independence.

I thank God and every lover of liberty down through the ages for that Flag.

The Flag is our heritage today because patriots, in every land of every age, have made the supreme sacrifice by giving up their lives for the sacred cause of liberty.

This heritage has now become our responsibility.

Let us not forget that the American Flag can be perpetuated only by eternal vigilance.

May we heed the entreaty on Governor Bradford's tombstone in Plymouth, which reads, "What our forefathers with so much difficulty secured, do not basely relinquish." Let us be so grateful to our ancestors for our heritage that we will go beyond its mere preservation for the benefit of our posterity. May we nurture the tree of liberty, which has grown from the seeds which were sown at Bethlehem, until it becomes so perfect and strong that it will be a haven and a shelter not only to every person who lives beneath the Stars and Stripes, but also to every person who lives within the sphere of the silent influence and gentle warmth of our Flag.

To this end, and "with a firm reliance on the protection of divine Providence", let us "mutually pledge to each other our Lives, our Fortunes and our Sacred Honor."

CHAPTER SIX

THE ONE GREAT UNION

Before the year 1349 in England, labor had been ground into the earth. Before that time there had been no strife between capital and labor because labor was helpless. In the year 1349 the Black Death occurred in England. One-half of the population died.

The Black Death gave labor its first opportunity to bargain for higher wages, shorter hours and better working conditions.

Of all remedies proposed to keep the equilibrium between capital and labor, trade unionism is the most practical.

Up to the Twentieth Century the cause of labor languished in the United States. There was no national trade union in the United States until 1834 and this union disappeared in the panic of 1837. Trade unions did not flourish in the United States until after 1860.

It is important that our labor unions be preserved. But there is a larger and a greater union on this hemisphere. We have here a grand and sublime union. On this earth there is a majestic and noble union to which the civilized world must look,—that union of forty-eight states we call the United States of America.

That is the glorious union to which we all belong. That is the union to which we all owe our liberty. That is the union on which all other unions rest. That is the one union which must be preserved above all others. No one can be loyal to his own trade union, unless he is first loyal to the great union we call the United States of America. That is the union which must come first in our minds and hearts. Our hearts, our hopes, our prayers, our tears, our faith must be with that union.

Longfellow wisely said:

> "Sail on, O Ship of State!
> Sail on, O Union, strong and great!
> Humanity with all its fears,
> With all the hope of future years,
> Is hanging breathless on thy fate!"

How true the words of Longfellow are today.

CHAPTER SEVEN

LEADERSHIP

To be a leader, a man must have in some degree the qualities, attributes and characteristics which I shall name and discuss.

1. *Intelligence and Knowledge*

If a group of men go hunting for deer, the one who has the most knowledge about the particular area in which they are hunting and has the best ideas about how to locate the deer and where each man should be placed, becomes the natural leader of the group.

If a group of boys are playing football on a vacant lot and one of them becomes severely injured, the boy who has the most knowledge about first aid becomes the leader in that emergency.

No man can be a successful leader in any undertaking, in civil or military life, unless he has intelligence and a little more knowledge about the thing before him than his associates. No better example can be found than where a company of soldiers in battle have all their officers and non-commissioned officers killed. Those who are left in that situation will instinctively and without a second's hesitation follow the

private soldier who knows just what to do in that
emergency.

2. *Understanding of Men*

A leader knows his men. He knows their weakness
and their strength. He knows what each one can do
best. He knows where to place his men. A leader
knows the peculiar capability of each man under him.
If a leader should be a high officer, such as a General
or the head of a great industrial company, where it is
impossible to know every man in the ranks, that leader, to be successful, will know intimately his key men
and will know in what position each key man should
be placed.

3. *Courage*

No man need aspire to a position of leadership, unless he has that quality of the mind and spirit we call
courage. This is a quality that cannot be cultivated
so much as many other attributes of leadership. A
man's courage is perhaps determined largely by his
ancestors. He may be under adverse conditions, in
danger, encounter difficulties. He may be what we
call afraid or scared. He may have some fear; but unless he has that quality of mind and soul we call
courage, which enables him to overcome all these and
push forward, he should be taken out of a position

of leadership. He is not a leader. I should like to cite Stonewall Jackson as perhaps our most courageous military leader.

4. *Initiative*

A leader, time and again, is called upon to institute a new course of action. It may be some course of action that has never been undertaken before. This is especially true of military leaders. General Marshall gave Major General Eisenhower orders to initiate a plan for crossing the English Channel and for invading France. He did such a good job; he showed that quality of initiative to such a high degree that General Marshall asked him whom he wanted to help him carry out his plan for crossing the Channel and invading France. This initiative, as well as initiative which General Eisenhower had shown many times before, made him the Commander of all the armies in the European Theater of war.

5. *Good Judgment*

Good judgment involves comparison and discrimination; it involves values and the relation of one thing to another on the part of a leader. To use good judgment a leader must first have knowledge enough to see the whole picture of the thing about which he is called upon to make a decision. The best example, in my opinion, of the use of good judgment in this war was the decision to defeat Germany first; the decision to throw the large part of our military power against Germany rather than Japan and rather than divide our military power equally against Germany and Japan. I think such leaders as President Roosevelt, Prime Minister Churchill, General Marshall, General Eisenhower and many other leaders are using good judgment in this respect.

6. *Enthusiasm*

No one can lead who is indifferent. Indifference never leads armies that conquer. Enthusiasm is contagious. A leader who has it passes it on to his followers. General George S. Patton, Jr. is a master at giving enthusiasm to those under his command. Guadalcanal could not have been taken at the time it was captured if the leaders had not filled the soldiers with enthusiasm for the task before them. The American people could not have produced the materials of war as they did if they had lacked enthusiasm. That enthusiasm was created by those who led, both among the military forces and in civilian life.

Every great moment in the history of the world is the result of the enthusiasm of some powerful leader. A successful leader loses himself in his leadership. He becomes a tonic to those who follow him. Enthusiasm is the crown of leadership.

7. *Obedience*

No man can command others unless he has first learned to obey commands. A soldier must first learn to obey his superiors before he is in a position to command obedience. During the great depression, an army of hungry veterans of the First World War marched on Washington. Herbert Hoover was President of the United States and as such was Commander-in-Chief of the Army. As Commander-in-Chief he ordered General Douglas A. MacArthur to disperse these hungry veterans. They may have had a just cause. The order may have been wrong. I have read that General MacArthur disliked the task he had been ordered to perform. General MacArthur performed the task with efficiency because, as a soldier, he had learned to obey the orders of his superior officers. He knows how to command obedience because he knows how to obey. That is one reason General MacArthur is a good leader.

8. *Resourcefulness*

A successful leader is resourceful. He may suddenly find himself in a position of peril. He may be surrounded by the enemy. A sudden emergency may arise. He must immediately devise ways to extricate himself and his followers.

The French Underground is succeeding against the

Germans because it has leaders who are resourceful in fooling them.

General MacArthur was resourceful in gaining time for America to prepare, when he retreated to the Peninsula of Bataan. He gained for America at least three months' time, threw the Japs' time-table off. The resourcefulness of General MacArthur may have won this war.

MacArthur proved his great leadership by his resourcefulness.

9. *Honor*

Just as a leader must learn to obey before he can command obedience, so he must also have honor if he wishes his followers to honor and respect him. I shall name Robert E. Lee as the outstanding leader of honor. He was dignified, kindhearted and a gentleman. He was a man of high character and was willing to sacrifice in the interest of his cause and in the interest of the men under his command. He had such calm dignity and was so courteous that he was loved by his soldiers. He was a man of honor and that was one of his main qualities of leadership.

10. *Coolness under Difficulties*

If a leader loses his head or gets excited when difficulties arise, he is not a good leader. The best example I have heard of a leader who was "cool headed" under the most extreme difficulties was the statement of General Wainwright, after General MacArthur left for Australia and the Jap General demanded that General Wainwright surrender Corregidor. That statement was: "They didn't teach me how to surrender at West Point, so I guess we'll have to fight on." He did fight on for some time and gained more precious time for the United States to prepare.

I think also that the answer of General McAuliffe, the leader of the detachment who was surrounded at Bastogne when he sent back a message to the German Commander who demanded that he surrender, which message consisted of the one word, "nuts," is a good example of coolness under difficulties.

These, to my mind, are examples of good leadership.

11. *An Iron Will*

Some one has said that the iron will of one stout heart shall make a thousand quail. The world is ruled by firm and decisive spirits. The power of the will annihilates difficulties. When a leader has made a firm resolve to obtain a certain end, the battle is half won. Other men stand aside for the man who has a determined will. A man who has a determination which knows no defeat is well on his way to victory.

The American soldiers who landed at Tarawa, and who had thousands of their men killed before they gained a foothold, must have had leaders with iron wills, or they never would have kept going.

To my mind, George Washington is the best example of a great leader with an iron will. He never wavered, although he met every kind of disappointment. His militia deserted. Congress had no power to raise money to prosecute a war. It was undoubtedly the iron will of Washington which gave us victory in the Revolutionary War.

I have no doubt that it was the iron will of Winston Churchill which saved England, and perhaps the world from slavery in the early part of the war. He expressed that iron will when he said: "We will fight them on the beaches. We will fight them in the streets. We will fight them on the landing fields. We will fight them in the fields. We will not surrender."

A leader cannot be a great leader without an iron will.

12. *Personality*

Personality is the last attribute of leadership I shall mention. Although I mention it last, it may be the most important. It is subtle. It is a divine gift. The leader who possesses personality to a high degree creates an atmosphere among those who follow him. That personality gives those under his comand a sense of enlargement. It unlocks possibilities and powers in soldiers they did not know they had. It gives them a new power. It draws out the best that is in his men. It makes soldiers like to obey orders of their leader. It doubles their strength and their powers. Leaders with great personalities make new men of those who follow while they are under the spell and in the atmosphere of that personality.

We have examples of such personalities among the officers who train us to be soldiers. We find Lieutenants, Captains, Majors and Colonels who have the personality and have the influence on us I have just mentioned.

I think our national military heroes who have created this atmosphere among their soldiers to the greatest degree are Washington, Lee, Pershing, MacArthur and Eisenhower.

CHAPTER EIGHT

GEORGE WASHINGTON, THE MAN OF
THE HOUR

Did you ever think that the Revolutionary stock had been in the process of making for a longer period than this country has existed since the Revolutionary War? Well, it had. The American of the Revolution had back of him the experience of 168 years in the wilderness of America. Most of the families traced their American ancestry back four or five generations. The people of that time thought of themselves as modern. They spoke of the "early days". The people of the Revolution looked back to Captain John Smith and Pocahontas, Miles Standish and Priscilla Alden, Roger Williams and Peter Stuyvesant through more of a haze than we look through to the historical characters of the Revolutionary period.

All of the white population in the colonies at the time of the Revolution grew from a total immigration of only one hundred thousand people. The population of the colonies at that time constituted the most thoroughly American stock that has ever inhabited the American continent. That is our stock. We are descended from that American blood.

The patriots of the Revolutionary Period constituted the flower of American civilization over a period
of 168 years. On this day and in this crisis, it will
be an inspiration to examine one product of that civilization.

On a February morning in 1732 a baby boy was
born in Virginia, not far from the blue water of the
Potomac. He opened his eyes in a four room house
which had two enormous chimneys, one at each end.
That house was surrounded by tangled forests in
which were interspersed fresh clearings, spotted with
innumerable stumps. The only connection that house
had with the outside world was by means of a narrow, rutty, muddy road.

They named that baby George; and his mother's
name was Mary Ball Washington. He spent his early
childhood in a crowded household.

His great grandfather, John Washington, came to
Virginia in 1657. He was a gentleman and an adven-
turer. He became a member of the Virginia Legisla-
ture and a Colonel of the Virginia Militia. His father,
Augustine Washington, attended school in England.
He owned considerable land, and was a business man.

At that time there were only two classes in Virginia. The aristocratic class included those who governed.
All others, including the backwoodsmen, made up the
other class. There was no middle class. George Wash-

ington had the unusual distinction of being born into a family which belonged to both classes. He was both an aristocrat and a backwoodsman. He remained both all his life.

George Washington never went to a public school, because there was none near his home. He studied under two tutors. He was not educated up to the average level of the aristocratic class, and he was far better educated than the average of the backwoodsmen.

When George was eleven years old, his father died. His oldest brother, Lawrence, had been away to the wars as an officer in the King's Army. George had seen him in his beautiful uniform when he came home, and had heard him tell of his experience in the wars.

When George was thirteen years old, he went to live with Lawrence. Lawrence was fourteen years older than George. Lawrence was well educated. He had studied in England. He was an aristocrat. He was George's glittering hero. Lawrence's home was called Mount Vernon. He had named it that in honor of Admiral Vernon under whom he had served in the war. That is the home which has now become one of the shrines of America.

At Mount Vernon George Washington met and talked with the aristocrats of Virginia, and the royalty and dignitaries from England. He met Lord Fairfax, a nobleman from England, who had inherited from his grandfather, Lord Culpeper, five million four hundred thousand acres of land in Virginia. George became a youthful favorite of Lord Fairfax, and at the age of sixteen, Fairfax gave him a job surveying his vast estate.

At the age of sixteen Washington left, temporarily, the pompous, chivalrous, colonial high life for the backwoods again. At that early age he had walked and talked with the royalty of England, and with the best aristocracy of Colonial Virginia. He knew the backwoods. We shall see, with the words of Kipling in mind, whether he had kept his virtue, or lost the common touch.

At sixteen Washington started out on what he thought was his life's work, that of a surveyor. It was at that age that he was appointed surveyor of Culpeper County. Surveying was one of the high and honored professions at that time in Colonial Virginia.

Washington at that time knew more mathematics than the average college graduate of today. He made good as a surveyor. The records shows that his surveys were all drawn and annotated in an orderly and neat manner.

When Washington was only twenty, his brother Lawrence died, leaving him a reversionary interest in the Mount Vernon estate, which came to him absolutely in a few years. But by this time George had earned money enough to buy and pay for 1558 acres of land in Virginia.

When his brother Lawrence died, George was appointed Adjutant General of Virginia, with the rank of Major. He was then twenty years of age.

Washington has now reached the place where he is about to undertake a task which starts him on a military career. There is a dispute between the English and the French over the territory along the Ohio River. Governor Dinwiddie of Virginia decides to send a message to the French Commander in that territory demanding that he evacuate that region immediately. The Governor sends his message by another Virginian who fails to reach the French forces because of the wilderness and the Indian savages. He returns, reports his failure, and goes into obscurity.

The Governor decides to select Major George Washington to carry the message. There is heroism in that job now. One man has failed. The French forces are three hundred miles away. That trip is like traveling through the jungles of Africa, with Indian savages thrown in. Washington is twenty-one years of age. He is now a rich young man. He can remain in the quiet and beauty of the Mount Vernon home. He can have ease and all the pleasures of life there.

But instead of this, he is willing and eager to go. This is a job that takes undaunted courage. It is like carrying a message to "Garcia" in these modern days. It has the elements of heroism in it.

But before he starts on this task, let us see what this young man of twenty-one looks like. What sort of a fellow is this mixture of aristocrat and backwoodsman?

He is six feet two inches tall; weighs 200 pounds, and is all muscle and bone. He wears size thirteen shoes and has massive hands, the largest in the Colony of Virginia. He is straight as an Indian. He has a strong chin, firm lips, blue-gray penetrating eyes, a superb neck, long legs and arms, a long face, high cheek bones, and a large mouth. He has an attractive smile, and a majestic walk. He is modest, and has an air of dignity and reserve. His step is firm; his carriage noble; and his personality graceful and commanding.

Washington set out on this long hazardous journey October 31, 1753. He was successful. He delivered his message to the French Commander. He used unusual diplomacy with the Indian chiefs for a youth of twenty-one. He returned through the snowdrifts of the Allegheny Mountains, after he had almost lost his life in the ice floes of the Ohio River, and after he had been the target of the Indians in the forest. The report of this journey was sent to England. At the age of twenty-one Washington was being discussed on the streets of London.

He had become the hero of his time. From that time, at the age of twenty-one, until his death, he was the man of the hour in the Colonies, and in the new nation.

We see him at twenty-three taking the command, after General Braddock is mortally wounded; we see him holding back the enemy with his Virginians, while the wreck of Braddock's Army runs to safety; we see him sitting on his third horse, with four bullet holes through his clothes, after two horses have been shot from under him.

We know he was appointed Commander of all the Virginia forces at the age of twenty-three; that later he became Commander-in-Chief of the Continental Army, and declined to accept any pay for his services. We know that in the struggle for independence that thousands continued to hold allegiance to Great Britain, and that thousands deserted from the Continental Army. We know he had Herculean problems with which to cope.

We see him cross the Delaware on Christmas night, 1776, while it is covered with ice floes, surprise the English, and win the battle of Trenton. We see him spend the terrible winter at Valley Forge.

We see him in action at Monmouth, and hear La-
fayette say of him: "I took time amid the roar and
confusion of the conflict to admire our beloved Chief,
who, mounted on a splendid charger, rode along the
ranks amid the shouts of the soldiers, cheering them
by his voice and example, and restoring to our standards the fortunes of the fight. I thought then, as now,
that never had I beheld so superb a man."

We see the village of Yorktown crumbling beneath
the feet of Cornwallis; British ships burning; trenches
taken; forts falling. We see Cornwallis surrender. The
Revolution is over, after six years of fighting. The
Declaration of Independence has now ripened into
independence for the Colonies.

Washington's activities were not confined to war.

He was one of the first American agriculturists. He
was one of the first conservationists in America.

He was a pioneer in American finance; a leading
business man of his day. He conducted fisheries,
drained swamps, built roads, planned canals, organized
companies and encouraged settlements.

The war was over, but Washington was still the
guiding star of the Colonies. The Colonies had gained
their independence, but they were still thirteen quar-
reling states, loosely bound together. Washington
presided over the Constitutional Convention in Philadelphia, where the Constitution was written. A vast

number of people were opposed to it. Its enemies referred to it in derision as that "New Plan".

Giants lived at that time, but Washington was a giant among giants. Thomas Jefferson, John Marshall, Alexander Hamilton, Benjamin Franklin, James Madison, George Wythe, Governor Randolph, Richard Henry Lee, Robert Morris, and all the other notables of that time respected him, and most of them looked to him for leadership. Without his influence the Constitution never would have been adopted.

A nation emerged under his leadership. He became the first President of the United States. He charted the course of this nation for the future. He became the Father of his country; first in war, first in peace, and first in the hearts of his countrymen. The eyes of the world were turned toward him.

Thomas Jefferson said of him:

"His integrity was most pure, his justice the most inflexible I have ever known, no motives of interest or consanguinity or friendship or hatred, being able to bias his decision. He was indeed in every sense of the word, a wise, a good, and a great man."

Those were the words of Thomas Jefferson. I say by whatever test we measure him he was a great man, one of the greatest this world has produced, if not the greatest.

But what I am most interested in is the reason for his greatness. He had a good ancestry, but no better than most of us. He was educated, but not as well as many of us today. He was physically strong, but his constitution was not as good as some of ours, for he had many sick spells. He lived in an unusual age, but so do we. Opportunities came to him, and so do opportunities stand outside our doors every day, and bid us wake and rise to fight and win. I believe he was lucky, and sometimes I feel that he must have had a guardian angel hovering over him; but we all have some luck, and as we look back over our lives, we are persuaded that there have been times when a guardian angel hovered over us.

He had a commanding personality; but he had his faults and his weaknesses, and his despairs and disappointments, just as we do.

He was honest and kind. He was polite and courteous. He was industrious. He had perseverance and a devotion to duty. But above all of these, I have come to the conclusion that George Washington owes his place in history to three things:

First, he was a curious mixture of aristocracy and the backwoods. He had the ability to keep that sturdy spirit of the backwoods and at the same time acquire the courtesy, and politeness and the polish of the first

families of Virginia. In him the two united. Both the
backwoods and aristocracy followed his leadership,
for he belonged to both.

He talked with crowds and kept his virtue. He
walked with kings and never lost the common touch.

Second, because he had a total lack of fear.
Throughout his whole life, he was cool in the presence
of danger. No man can be a great leader, unless he
is gifted with that attribute.

Third, he had a great love for his country. He was
willing to sacrifice for it. He was willing to give up
everything for its welfare. He put his country above
everything else.

Let us all emulate the example set by that product
of the flower of American civilization.

PART III

VICE

PART III

VICE

CHAPTER NINE

JUST ANOTHER DRUNKARD

God has made it possible for man to have every kind of thrill and pleasure. For the eye He has given man the sunrise and the sunset, the flowers, the green pastures and the landscapes. For the ear He has given man the songs of the birds and beautiful music. For the palate He has covered the earth with food. For man's inner nature He has given him his associations, his family, his work and his play. He has given man a brain that takes him into the spirit and the dream world. Man can enjoy everything that God has given him, and not have a headache or a "hangover" the next morning.

But man, with all his ingenuity, thinks he can improve on the work of God. Man figured out a way to make liquor. God had nothing to do with this. Man sometimes thinks he is wiser than Nature. He thinks he needs a thrill that is not natural, and he takes a drink. It exhilarates him. His blood moves faster.

His heart works harder. He gets grandiose ideas. He
thinks he is the best man in the world. He says, "on
with the dance; let joy be unconfined." The liquor he
has taken has done nothing more than build a fire in his
system. For a while he feels its warmth, but to sustain
the warmth he must continue to pour the fuel on the
fire. After a while he begins to get a jittery feeling,
because the ashes from the fire begin to pile up so deep
that the fire fails to burn with its former brilliance.
When this time comes, he thinks he has to "taper off".
He does not have the nerve to take the consequences.
He knows what the consequences are, for he has done
this same thing before; but he beguiles himself into be-
lieving he knows how to do it this time. He starts on
the "tapering off" process, but he is only putting more
oil on the fire. His stomach finally gets so indignant
at this cruel and inhuman treatment it has been receiv-
ing, that it revolts and refuses to take any more. That
is when he has to quit. He is worse off than when he
started to "taper off". The awful realization is on him
that finally he must go through the suffering. He
would not do it, if he had any choice; but he has no
choice. His "hangover" is on. He has gastritis in his
belly; quivers in his stomach; palpitation in his heart;
pain in his head; jagged and jittery nerves, inside and
out; depression in his mind; and grouch in his dispo-
sition.

He thinks he will die, and is afraid he will not. His appetite is gone, but he could not eat if he had one. Kind Old Nature, which he has brutally abused, starts to work again for him, as soon as he stops pouring in the poison: but Nature's work is slow. The minutes seem like hours. He will recover, if his heart is strong enough, and he has not continued his drinks long enough to get delirium tremens.

He does not understand what has happened to him. When he was in the twenties, he "got away" with it. Youth threw the poison off then. He cannot "take it" now, and wonders why. After a day or so he finally comes out of it. He appreciates the natural feelings of life. He swears off, and says he is done. But after so long a time he begins to deceive himself again. He decides he is drinking the wrong brand. He changes the brand and still he cannot "take it". Then he remembers that corn never did agree with him. He changes from bourbon to rye whiskey, but he gets no better result. Then he buys better and more expensive liquor, and again there is disappointment. The reason is that regardless of the cost, he is not young any more, and all liquor has alcohol in it. He did not "get away with it" when he was in the "twenties". John Barleycorn was only leading him on.

John Barleycorn has got the best of them. He has taken his toll of athletes, prizefighters, lumber jacks, and those in all trades and professions. He has got brilliant statesmen, soldiers, poets, geniuses, and even judges. They have all thought they could "lick" Old John. He has laid them all low, and laughed at them. He will get anyone who trifles with him long enough.

Yes, anyone who trifles with John Barleycorn long enough will awaken some day to find that he has insulted his friends, mistreated his wife, neglected his children and his job, disgusted everybody, and made a nuisance of himself. He will realize that he has wallowed in the mud like a hog. The terrible realization will come over him that he is just another drunkard,— a common drunkard.

CHAPTER TEN

THE TWIN SABOTEURS

Gentlemen of the Grand Jury:

The relationship between the sexes is one of the most beautiful and the finest that has been given to the human race, if that relationship is under the proper circumstances and in accordance with the approved customs of the Christian world, which have existed since the time of Moses. But the commercialization of that beautiful relationship has become one of the curses of the modern world. Largely because of that commercialization, the twin saboteurs, syphilis and gonorrhea, are rapidly destroying the life blood of America.

The sex instinct is powerful, and for this reason it is easily exploitable for financial gain. Commercialized vice is a big business in the United States. Statistics show that the girl who is the victim of this vice is usually feeble-minded. Her share of the profits is small. She seldom has more than a mere existence. She is an outcast. She is arrested, fined and turned loose to ply her trade again. Punishment of the girl does not destroy prostitution.

The foundation of prostitution is profits,—profits to owners of property, hotel keepers, innkeepers, matrons, managers, runners, feelers, panderers, and pimps. The law must reach out and get these men and women.

Houses of prostitution are reservoirs of syphilis infection. In the Middle Ages syphilis was called the "Great Pox" in contrast to smallpox. We have practically conquered smallpox. We can and must conquer the "Great Pox", which is far more destructive.

If typhoid fever should break out in any community, the people would immediately ascertain the origin of the typhoid germs, and eliminate the source. Yet in America, reservoirs of syphilis infection are permitted to exist. We know where most of these reservoirs are. We know their existence is illegal, and yet they continue to exist.

Not all syphilis comes from houses of prostitution, but syphilis can never be conquered as long as houses of prostitution exist, any more than a typhoid epidemic can be conquered if a water well, polluted with typhoid germs, is left along a public highway where those who are thirsty can quench their thirst. And this is especially true if it is profitable for someone to have lots of water drunk from this well, and he hires some "dead beats" about town, better known as pimps, to tell the young fellows growing up, and some old ones, too, that this is very fine water, and then shows the boys where it is. Then how true this is if this same fellow who profits by this well has it tested for everything except typhoid germs, and gives out the information that it has been found to be pure water.

Gentlemen, am I talking about something that is serious or not? Let us look facts straight in the face. The most conservative statistics show that there are thirteen million people in the United States who are infected with syphilis,—one out of every ten. Some authorities put it much higher than that. There are 600,000 new cases every year in this great country of ours. Syphilis is doing one hundred times as much damage in the United States as infantile paralysis. It is disabling five times as many people as automobile accidents. From three per cent to five per cent of all children born are born with syphilis. It is as devastating as leprosy, or an epidemic of cholera. It is more destructive than cancer, and in many cases, medical authorities believe, causes cancer. There is twice as much syphilis in the United States as scarlet fever, thirteen times as much as diphtheria, and twenty-eight times as much as typhoid fever.

Our health departments over the country treat many times as much syphilis as all other acute communicable diseases combined. Many pregnant women have syphilis. Some of them receive medical treatment for it, and some do not. Those who are treated, if the treatment starts early in pregnancy, have a good chance of giving birth to a healthy child. Those who do not receive medical treatment are almost certain to give birth to a syphilitic child.

Ninety per cent of all cases of syphilis could be cured, if properly treated and treated at the proper time.

Syphilis is acquired in four ways: first, by sexual contact; second, by kissing individuals who have it; third, in rare cases by indirect contact, such as drinking cups, pipes, and so forth, on which the germ exists, —the germ of syphilis can only live on moist surfaces; fourth, by inheritance.

Syphilis is called the "Great Deceiver". Many people have diseases of the various organs of the body called by various names which are caused by syphilis. Eighteen per cent of all heart diseases comes from syphilis. The following diseases are some of the diseases which are often caused by syphilis: angina pectoris, apoplexy, locomotor ataxia, general paresis (this is a softening of the brain, and is one form of insanity), deformed bodies, blindness, deafness, paralysis, and ugly sores.

More than commercial prostitutes are involved in this problem of eradicating syphilis. Statistics show that commercial prostitutes are directly responsible for twenty-five per cent of the problem. Clandestine affairs are responsible for twenty-five per cent of the problem. And fifty per cent of those who have syphilis are innocently infected. Husbands are innocently infected by wives. Wives are innocently infected by husbands. The new born babe is innocently infected by the mother,—this is called congenital or inherited syphilis. This syphilis inherited by the baby is very contagious and other members of the family or friends may become infected.

In the 9th verse of the Fifth Chapter of Deuteronomy we find the statement: "The Lord thy God am a jealous God, visiting the iniquities of the fathers upon the children unto the third and fourth generation." This is not only a Bible statement; this is a statement of a scientific fact, and it is particularly true of syphilis.

Syphilis strikes with more deadly force than a hundred-horsepower automobile running at a terrific rate of speed. If it connects with your grandfather, your child's body may be twisted and its brain destroyed from the vibrations.

Dr. Thomas Parran, Surgeon General of the United States Public Health Service, in showing how deceitful syphilis is, says that in many cases "nothing at all is suspected until the awful period at which the late syphilis appears; perhaps when a syphilitic baby is born; perhaps when life insurance is refused because of organic heart disease. Perhaps the stumbling gait of locomotor ataxia, the irritability and delusions of general paresis, or failure of vision preceding total blindness first brings knowledge of the mad-dog infection which has, at last, a strangle hold,—and which may turn its victim into a white-faced invalid with damaged heart and blood vessels, a derelict whose face is eaten by great sores, or a homicidal maniac behind barred windows."

General Pershing said: "I regard syphilis as the most terrible scourge that afflicts mankind."

He further said: "In this war on syphilis, all must work at it intelligently according to their opportunity and their ability to take part in it, and they must do so with the old war-time spirit that defeated the enemy in 1918. It is most encouraging to know that the American Legion with its 12,000 posts is taking an active part in this movement."

Syphilis is the next plague that must be eliminated. This scourge should be ended within this generation. We must have an aroused public. We must break the hold this disease has on human life in this country.

Gonorrhea is the twin peril of syphilis, although there is no connection between the two diseases, except that they are both venereal diseases. Gonorrhea never develops into syphilis. Many people have both diseases at the same time.

The Remedy

What is the most effective way to cope with these two most effective saboteurs? Is segregation the most effective way to deal with the terrible problem of syphilis and gonorrhea? Is it better for the law to recognize houses of ill fame and for the enforcement officers to keep them segregated in one part of the city and try to regulate them?

Our War Department found thirty years ago that segregation was not the remedy. The Navy, the Federal Security Agency, the International Association of Chiefs of Police and State Health Associations have come to the same conclusion at which the Army arrived. All of these departments and associations base their conclusions on hard facts and statistics.

Statistics show that segregated red light districts increase venereal diseases. In 1917 in a certain American city, its houses of prostitution were running wide open. Thousands of soldiers were located just outside the city. The venereal disease rate among the soldiers was 168 per thousand per year. Then vigorous policing closed the houses and made street walkers scarce. After fourteen months of this policy the venereal disease rate had dropped to five per thousand per year. With segregated open houses in that city venereal disease was thirty-one times what it was after fourteen months of no houses of prostitution and vigorous policing. There are hundreds of illustrations of this kind that could be given.

Disease increases where there is segregation because segregation increases the number of contacts with the individual carrier. All who are interested know just where to go where there is segregation.

Statistics show that most prostitutes are diseased. Let us suppose, however, that she is free from disease at the time she is examined. If the first customer who has contact with her after she has had an examination is infected, she may transmit the disease to every man from that time until the time of her next examination.

Prostitutes cannot protect their customers, as some believe. There is nothing the woman can use which will prevent infection of the man. Most prostitutes are mentally deficient and therefore do not have skill and knowledge as to protection.

When any community permits segregation of prostitutes, it is giving legal status to a vicious racket that is striking directly at its welfare and health. It is perpetuating a place that is the nerve center of crime.

When medical inspection is given to these harlots, while they continue their business of prostitution, which inspection, they, of course, advertise to their customers, and which inspection is known generally by the community, the result of this medical inspection does not protect, but only increases the business of the prostitutes. The net result of that inspection is an increase of disease because it results in more business and thus more contacts. The doctor then in making that inspection for active prostitutes, is unwittingly putting his stamp of approval on her as to safety, and giving the ignorant customers a false sense of security.

The records show that when any police force tries to segregate and regulate houses of ill fame, some of the police force, in time, becomes corrupt. Any police force that thinks it can regulate this racket successfully will wake up some day to find that its regulation is a failure and that the racket has control of the police force.

You can't eliminate a cesspool by throwing a blanket over it. You can't stop that cesspool from spreading disease by throwing police protection around it. Medical inspection will do the community no good, if the cesspool is left there.

The Wise Folks

But some of the so-called wise folks will throw their hands up and say that if the judge of this court has his way, we will have street walkers in Morgantown. When they say that, they base their conclusion on a false premise. They are assuming that where there is segregation, there are no street walkers. Nothing is farther from the facts. Records are against them. Statistics from numerous cities show that there are more clandestine prostitutes in cities which permit brothels than in cities which do not permit them. That is true of Morgantown today. This thriving city situated here on the banks of the placid and beautiful Monongahela River, with its great educational institutions, has more street walkers and clandestine prostitutes than at any other time in its history. The reason for that is that when enforcement officers do not vigorously enforce the law as to one phase of prostitution, they cannot very consistently enforce the law as to another phase of it. From now on the law must be enforced as to every kind and type of commercialized prostitution.

Say Sex Crimes Increase

There are a few people who say that sexual crimes will increase if the red light district is eliminated. Again statistics do not substantiate this belief. The opposite is true in most cities. After all, I have never heard of a brothel making a law-abiding citizen out of a criminal or a saint out of a fiend.

Say are Necessary

There are a few people, and some are sincere, who say that houses of ill fame are necessary. Let us examine that belief to see if it is sound. Who are those who frequent these houses?

The first class is made up of disgruntled married

men. They should stay at home where they belong.

The second group is made up of young men and boys. Here the responsibility of society is the heaviest. It is the youth of the country who suffer most from the scourge of venereal disease. Statistics show that of those who are treated for syphilis at clinics in West Virginia the average age is twenty years, and many of them are in the low "teens". In the name of childhood alone, everyone should join the fight against this scourge. Houses of prostitution are not only unnecessary for young men and boys, but they must be kept out of their reach, if this nation is to remain strong enough to survive in this mad world. We must protect the health of our youth, until they have properly developed.

The third class is made up of lonely men. Here the community must step in and give them recreation. There is a recreational center established in this war area by the Federal Government and the City of Morgantown. It is doing a remarkable work. I recommend it for this class of men. The churches and other organizations can help here.

We have taken the attitude of the ostrich as to the disease of syphilis. We can do this no longer. We must take our heads out of the sand and look this disease squarely in the face. When we do this, it can be conquered. It can be stamped out just as smallpox, typhoid fever, and diphtheria have largely been banished from the land. If we fail to do this immediately, it will conquer us, and our good old American race will be destroyed.

But the twin saboteurs are harder to stamp out than smallpox, because there are a lot of people who make profits out of businesses which flourish on habits and practices that help to spread syphilis and gonorrhea. It not only takes intelligence to stamp out these diseases, it takes courage and honesty on the part of public officials, health officers, the medical profession, grand juries, petit juries, and the good people in general.

Must not Treat Merely as Crime

We cannot stamp out this disease by merely treating it as a crime. It must also be treated as a disease. This problem always becomes more acute in war time. The soldiers are always the worst victims. This was true in the Civil War, and the first World War. It is true today.

Our Duty

We have a duty here to perform the same as General MacArthur and his men have in the Pacific. We can't shirk while men die. We are all fighting in the same cause. A public officer on the home front has no more right to neglect his duty than a soldier on Bataan Peninsula. We have the same obligation to be cou-

rageous as they have. We must eliminate everything
that weakens our nation; it is in peril; its very existence
is at stake.

This is a community problem. It is a state problem.
It is a national problem. The local communities, the
various states, and the National Government must cooperate in solving it.

The American is the noblest production of time; he
is the result of the progress of the ages; he represents
the best that every Christian generation has produced.
America has a great heritage; but it also has great responsibilities. This has been a virile nation. We must
keep it that way. This nation is the guardian of the
liberty of the world. It is the protector against foreign
invasion of the nations of two continents. This nation
must be strong and healthy and vigorous, if it expects
to fulfill its mission.

As judge of this court, I call to this cause, not only
the assistance of the prosecuting attorney, this grand
jury, and all enforcement officers, but also the news-
papers, the American Legion, the Veterans of Foreign
Wars, Women's Clubs, the Service Clubs, the professions of medicine, law, religion, and education, including parent-teachers associations, and all governmental
departments, and all the forces of science and sociol-
ogy. I call on an aroused public to assist in stamping
this disease out of America within this generation.

CHAPTER ELEVEN

THE LOVE OF MONEY

As Judge of this Court, I feel a strong sense of duty to call to the attention of this Grand Jury, and to the attention of the good people of this County, some conditions that are existing as to gambling.

Blackstone says: "Gambling is a kind of tacit confession that those engaged therein, in general, exceed the bounds of their respective fortunes; and therefore they cast lots to determine on whom the ruin shall at present fall, that the rest may be saved a little longer."

Benjamin Franklin said: "Keep flax from fire and youth from gambling."

George Washington once said: "Gambling is the child of avarice, the brother of iniquity, and the father of mischief."

Dryden said: "Bets, at the first, were fool-traps, where the wise, like spiders, lay in ambush for the flies."

Solomon said: "He that maketh haste to be rich shall not be innocent."

I am not condemning so much a friendly game of cards. I am condemning that kind of gambling that takes money from a whole community and enriches a few.   I am speaking of that gambling that takes from the pockets of the poor, and makes richer the already rich.   I am condemning that gambling which takes money from fathers which they should have spent on milk for their babies.

I request that the enforcement officers continue their war on the gambling dens in this City until they are broken up. People in this County have come to me and said, can't something be done about these gambling dens? They have made remarks as follows: "My boy was all right until he got in the habit of going there. My son-in-law is neglecting his wife and baby. He stays out all night in those gambling dens. My husband is going to the bad in these gambling dens,—he used to stay home nights with me and the children; now he spends his time at the gambling dens." A boy came in crying and said: "Judge, I want to talk to you about my pa. He used to take care of ma and us kids. He don't do it no more.   He stays down at that gambling joint."

People are not rich enough to gamble. What this County needs is the spirit of frugality and industry.

A poet once said: "No man e'er found a happy life by chance; or yawned it into being with a wish."

I say, as Judge of this Court, that no community will ever be prosperous and happy, if it desires to make a living by chance instead of work.

No man has a right to gamble away his baby's milk; he has no right to gamble his child's health; he has no right to gamble his son's or daughter's future.

In the sixth chapter of Timothy, St. Paul said: "But they that will be rich, fall into temptation, and a snare, and into many foolish and hurtful lusts, which drown men in destruction and perdition.

"For the love of money is the root of all evil; which while some coveted after, they have erred from the faith, and pierced themselves through with many sorrows."

St. Paul here does not refer to money as the root of all evil; he says that the love of money is the root of all evil.

Some say, well, people have the gambling instinct and will gamble regardless of what the enforcement officers do. I think it is true that many people do have the gambling instinct. That fact is the very reason that some people who cannot afford to lose any money need protection. The money a man has, does not belong to him to gamble away, until he has fed his children.

CHAPTER TWELVE

PANHANDLERS

The good people of this community are being preyed upon and annoyed by a group of panhandlers. This must stop. There is no logical reason for it. We have organized relief now to take care of those who are worthy. These panhandlers are a group of worthless, wretched "dead-beats" who are begging, not for the purpose of helping themselves, but for the purpose of further debauching themselves and making themselves more foul and filthy. They are not begging to get money to buy bread; they are begging to get money to buy rotten concoctions to drink, so that they can further destroy their minds and bodies.

Giving to these panhandlers is not charity; it is weakness; it is stupid and pusillanimous. The public perpetuates these panhandlers and "dead-beats" by giving them pennies, nickels, dimes, and quarters. They not only should not be fostered, because fostering them ruins themselves, but because they are a menace to the health and morals of a community. Any one who fosters this group by giving them money is not a good citizen.

CHAPTER THIRTEEN

OBSCENE PICTURES

Any obscene literature or pictures which are sold in any community usually gets into the hands of the youth. If someone should poison this community's water supply or its food supply, and someone died, that, of course, would be murder. But poison in the stomach is soon detected. We have many able physicians who can pump poison out of the stomach, or give an antidote to counteract its effect. But if someone poisons the mind of your child with dirty, foul and obscene literature and pictures, you may not know about it. No one may know it at first. That is a slow kind of poison. And after you discover it, what are you going to do about it? You can't pump that poison out. That kind of poison not only permeates the brain cells of the child; it pollutes his mind and soul. You will not find a doctor who can cure that disease.

We must protect the morals of our children until they have properly developed. It is the duty of society to place about youth an environment that will help them to live in obedience to natural law. The sex element must be preserved in the growing child. It is this element in the growing child, which, if preserved and properly directed, that rounds out his physical development; gives solidity to his muscles; elasticity to his step; animation to his expression; vigor to his energies; keenness to his intellect; courage to his convictions; and stability to his character.

Dissipate and weaken the sex powers in youth, and every feeling, emotion, and sentiment will have lost a vivacious thrill they otherwise would have had. Obscene, dirty and foul literature and pictures can have no other effect than that of dissipating the sex powers of our children, depriving them of a magnetic personality, and destroying the usefulness of many of them in the future.

CHAPTER FOURTEEN

DRIVING DRUNK

More than ninety per cent of all crimes committed in this county, with the exception of driving drunk, are committed by a very small percentage of our population, and by people who by reason of heredity, environment or some other reason, never have been heard of in the county, until some newspaper blazons their names on its front page, after they have committed some crime.

But what of drunken drivers? More than ninety per cent of the drunken driving in this county is done by people who, in all other respects, are good citizens; by people who are intelligent, who stand high in their community; many of whom have nice families, trades, professions, and some of whom hold high positions. This seems like an anomaly in the history of crime. It is particularly anomalous, when we realize the seriousness of the crime of driving drunk.

Very few of those who drive drunk would go into a five-and-ten-cent store and surreptitiously slip a five-cent article into their pockets. Here the question of the physical injury to a human being, or the destroying of human life does not enter. Yet the same individual who would never for one minute entertain a thought of stealing that five-cent article, and would be in favor of prosecuting anyone who did such a thing, will go to a road house, a dance, a party or some other convenient place, fill himself up with liquor, and in that condition step into his one hundred horsepower automobile, seat himself behind the steering wheel, and with the liquor causing his heart to pump the blood to his brain twice as rapidly as normal, turn on that one hundred horsepower engine. There he sits, commander of a powerful and complex machine,—starter, clutch, gear shift, brakes, steering wheel and lights, all to look after. In that condition he turns that powerful machine into a busy public highway. If he does not hit someone when he turns into the highway, he proceeds along that highway with a two-cylinder brain instead of six, filled with short circuits, causing his vision to be blurred and confused, and his muscles to lack coordination. He is lucky if he does not kill someone on the highway, including himself and the occupants of his car.

If he should shoot a high-powered rifle up a busy street, he would be lucky if he did not kill someone. If he did kill anyone, he would be guilty of murder in the first degree. A high-powered automobile on a busy highway, driven by a drunken driver, is analogous to the high-powered rifle, as far as the danger is concerned.

CHAPTER FIFTEEN

SEXUAL PERVERTS AND DEGENERATES

There are only two sure ways to cure a sexual degenerate. One way is with the noose, and the other way is with the surgeon's knife. He can only be cured with the noose, if he commits a capital offense. He cannot be cured with the surgeon's knife, because we have no law for it. Whatever degenerates there are in this community, whether they are floaters, or whether their permanent residence is here, must be taken out of society. They have no place in society. They are a constant and dangerous menace to our boys and girls. A sexual pervert is a dangerous criminal.

CHAPTER SIXTEEN

NO RIGHT TO LOOK A SKUNK IN
THE FACE

You have been indicted by the grand jurors of this county, because you enticed a six-year old girl out into the bushes and mistreated her, and committed degenerate acts in her presence.

It is fortunate for you, as far as your existence on this earth is concerned, that you did not inflict on this little child any noticeable external physical injury. If you had, you would have been sentenced under another law. Since you have not, you will be sentenced under the two indictments to which you have pleaded guilty, that of contributing to the delinquency of an infant, and that of assault.

Although you have not inflicted on this little child any noticeable external physical injury, you have violated a little child's delicate sense of decency; you have shocked the mechanism of her sensitive nervous system, from which she may never recover; you have planted in her heart a fear that may grow into an obsession, and take possession of her, as she develops into womanhood; you have damaged that cloak of innocence which God places around every child, and

which is so important to its future development and
welfare. You have astounded and outraged this community; you have violated the laws of nature; you have
violated the laws of civilization; you have even violated any brute instincts which you may have inherited; for the brutes do not commit such acts as those to
which you have pleaded guilty.

You are not fit to associate with other human beings. You have disgraced your father and mother; you
have disgraced your relatives; you have disgraced the
human race. God controls the animals through their
instincts. He put you on a higher plane. He gave you
the intelligence of a human being. He gave you the
right to choose between right and wrong. He gave
you the freedom of choice. He gave you an independent will. He gave you the power of reasoning. He
gave you two legs, instead of four, so that you could
stand upright and look the world in the face. He made
it possible for you to turn your eyes upward to the
stars. But you have deprived yourself of the right to
look even a skunk in the face.

You have committed a crime which is repulsive, dis-
gusting, nauseating, loathsome, shocking, detestable,
revolting, vile and damnable.

CHAPTER SEVENTEEN

LET GOD DO SOMETHING FOR YOU

You have been convicted of unlawful wounding. If you had been an exemplary citizen all your life you could be sentenced to five years in the State Penitentiary at Moundsville.

You have been a menace to this community for many years. You have violated the law numerous times. You have cost the taxpayers of this county thousands of dollars.

Your crimes have finally overtaken you. You are one of the worst characters this county has ever had to endure. The people of this community have been patient with you. At times I am astounded at the patience of good people. You have been given every chance to reform. Even when you were tried for this crime for which you are now about to be sentenced, American justice tenderly put around you every safeguard. The law required the judge of this court to appoint an attorney to represent you. This court did that. You were represented by an able attorney. When the jury was chosen you had six strikes and the state had only two. A jury of twelve of your neighbors decided whether or not you were guilty.

This court instructed them that, under the law, you were presumed to be innocent and that it was necessary for the State to prove you guilty beyond all reasonable doubt, before the jury could find you guilty. Every safeguard was thrown around you that would be thrown around a man who had lived a perfect life, and who was worth untold millions. Under American justice not even your rotten character could be brought in issue, and presented to the jury. The jury was even kind to you.

You have no one to blame except yourself. You have slowly but surely destroyed your own usefulness. You have indulged in crime, debauchery, degeneracy, loathsomeness and drunkenness.

You have been guilty of many of the crimes listed in the books. A partial survey of the records shows that you have been found guilty or pleaded guilty to forty crimes in this county. That list does not include an indictment for sodomy (a crime against nature) for which you were never tried because the judge of this court and the prosecuting attorney came to the conclusion that the acts which you were charged with committing were too low, vile, dirty, filthy, base, degenerate, rotten, and putrid to bring out before the public.

I would not insult a beast by calling you that. You do not belong in the class of beasts. They are on a much higher plane than you are.   You have slowly but surely dragged yourself down lower than the reptiles that crawl in filth and dirt and darkness.

Thank God this community is rid of you for awhile.

Your sentence is one to five years in the State Penitentiary at Moundsville at hard labor. The emphatic recommendation of this Court is that you serve the maximum of five years.   No credit will be given you for time served in the county jail.

Let us all hope that after you go to the penitentiary that you will let God do something for you. The Lord will help you, if you will give him a chance.

PART IV

WAR

PART IV

WAR

CHAPTER EIGHTEEN

THE DAWN OF AN OMINOUS YEAR

The people of America are standing today at the dawn of the ominous and dark year of 1941. The zero hour has arrived. There must be no tolerance, no patience, and no compromise with the forces of tyranny.

There is no use for us to beguile ourselves. We are in this world storm. We may call it neutrality, or non-belligerency, or an emergency, or war. By whatever name we call it, does not change the fact we are in this world struggle. We have no choice. The sooner we recognize this fact, the better off we will be.

In this year we must resolve to make ourselves stronger; to give rather than to get; to get rid of self indulgence; eliminate all softness and flabbiness in the mind and body; look facts squarely in the face; acquire again the old-fashioned virtues; have an abiding faith in what is right; look back to our ancestors for spiritual strength, to Valley Forge and Gettysburg;

look back to the companions of our youth who died in the first world struggle and draw strength from that reservoir filled with the spirit of human liberty, the emotions of courage, the examples of unselfishness, the pride of honor and the exemplification of all that is great and good in the American. Yes, draw strength, spiritual strength, from the legacy they left us.

CHAPTER NINETEEN

JOHNNY COMES MARCHING HOME

I want to say a word about Johnny to his parents. It seems only yesterday to you, when he was a tiny baby and you walked the floor with him up against your shoulder at night to cure him of the colic; when he for the first time found his toes and made good use of them; when you were frightened because you caught him making his first trip crawling up the steps; when he got out of your sight for the first time, and you were sure something terrible had happened to him; when he left you and was gone all day to school for the first time; when he failed to come in at night at the time you expected him, and you sat up anxiously waiting and letting your imagination make you believe everything bad had happened to him. To you that was only yesterday.

But Johnny grew up to be a strong broad-shouldered young man. His eyes were bright; his ears were keen; his muscles were elastic; his heart was strong; he carried in his veins the blood that he had inherited from three hundred years of fighting men, for he not only had inherited from the men who had fought victoriously in six major wars in one hundred and forty-two years, but he had also inherited from the intrepid men and women who had fought a three-hundred-years Indian war; and Johnny carried in his heart the best that every Christian generation had produced.

Any nation is looking for a boy like that, when it is in peril and its very existence is threatened. America was looking for Johnny and he went. He left you and his familiar surroundings, his school, his first job. He turned his back on young dreams and young love. He became a part of the most powerful war machine in the world.

He is not fighting on his home grounds. He is doing what you would expect him to do because of his inheritance; he is taking the fight to his enemies. He is fighting on his enemies' home grounds. His way there was fraught with dangers, for the oceans were infested with enemy submarines, and the air was filled with enemy bombers. He landed in a strange country and in a strange climate many thousands of miles from home. He fought exposure and disease.

Johnny has already proved to you that he can fight. The Japs asked for a fight, and he has already accommodated them. He defeated them in the air over the Coral Sea and on the Coral Sea. By this battle he saved Australia. He defeated the Japs again in the Midway Island area, and saved Hawaii and an invasion of the West Coast. He annihilated those cocky, slant-eyed, barbarous Jap-rats in the Bismarck Sea and knocked the whole Japanese nation reeling on its heels. The Japs, as dumb as they are, discovered at that time that when they met Johnny, they were up against a fighter that was too good for them.

He bombed Tokyo in his destructive sweep over Japan. He landed in the steaming, disease-infested jungles on Guadalcanal, slugged the Japs there into insensibility and hurled them from that island. He is gradually exterminating them on the Island of New Guinea.

This daring and unterrified Johnny landed on the cold, bleak, desolate, wild, dreary and fog-bound Island of Attu, utterly destroyed and exterminated the Japs there and captured that strategic island. By annihilating the Japs on the Island of Attu and by scaring them out of the Island of Kiska, he cleared the Aleutians of all Japs and started his country on its offensive way to the heart of Japan.

He swept across the sands of Northern Africa and the mud of Tunisia and decisively defeated the vaunted Africa Korps of Marshal Rommel. He crossed the Mediterranean and punctured the underbelly of the Fortress of Europe in Sicily.

This baby who only yesterday you were afraid would fall down the stairs and injure himself, steps on to the beach at Salerno while German artillery shoots at him and German tanks try to run over him. He stopped the tanks and silenced the artillery and is now inside the Fortress of Europe. Only a great fighter can do what he did there. No history will ever be more glorious than Johnny made when he landed and held the narrow beach at Salerno.

He has much fighting yet to do. He will still have to fight on other beaches of Europe, over the hills of Italy, along the mountains of China, in the jungles of the South Sea Islands. He will still have to fight on every front in the world, on land, at sea and in the air. He will win. Victory is in his blood. Johnny will come marching home to you, bringing you a military victory. To you he will still be just your baby. You will still see his dimpled hands and cheeks. You will still carry with you the tender memories of his childhood. You are not criticized for that; your reaction is natural because you are his father and mother.

But he will actually be much more than you will realize. He will be a man who has toiled and fought and suffered, endured exposure, experienced diseases, gone through discomforts, had disappointments, been embittered at times, felt loneliness, longed for a refreshing drink and a home-cooked meal, missed friends and all those near and dear to him. He will bring back to you a mind which has experienced excitement and thrills; a heart that has felt deep emotions; and a soul that has been enriched because he has walked with God on the firing line for his country and humanity.

He will bring back home a memory of the world,— its great oceans, its jungles, its cities, its peoples, its beauty and its ugliness, its cruelty and its kindness. He will have walked through the streets of Berlin and Tokyo. He will have walked down the Champs Elysees. He will have strolled through the Palace of Versailles. He will bring back a memory of the culture of Rome, of the beauty of Paris, of the glory of Athens. He will have walked and talked with peoples of many tongues.

Johnny will have loved and been loved. He will have hated and been hated. He will have thought long and seriously. From all of this he will come home with some definite conclusions, fixed ideas, and a sound philosophy of life.

Yes, he will bring you a military victory, but he cannot bring you a victorious peace. That is out of his power. A victorious peace depends on you. It depends on me. Those who remain at home are responsible for a victorious peace. They failed before. Will we fail this time?

CHAPTER TWENTY

THE HOME FRONT

We who are on the home front have a duty to perform the same as an American soldier in New Guinea, on Guadalcanal, or in North Africa. We cannot shirk while other men fight and die. An officer at home has no more right to neglect his duty than an American soldier on the Island of Attu. We have the same obligation to be courageous. We must keep the home front in order. We must eliminate everything that in any way weakens this nation.

Every officer, whether he has been elected or appointed, is a public character. All of his actions are closely scrutinized. It should not even be necessary for me to say that every enforcement officer, as well as all other officers, must be honest with the public; faithful to their trust; and loyal to American ideals. Every officer should be courageous enough to stand by the right, and where it is his duty he should be industrious enough to ferret out evil and eliminate it.

CHAPTER TWENTY-ONE

UNITED AND AROUSED

In spite of all we have done at home and in the far flung battle areas of the world we still hear talk about the apathy and lethargy and complacency of the American people. Those statements are no longer true. We are now a united people. We are an aroused people. We are ready to make all sacrifices necessary to win this war. All this talk that we are losing this war is silly talk. We haven't even come to bat yet. The greatest danger I see now is all this clamor for hasty victory. This nation should not strike until it is ready. When it is ready and it does strike, it will not only surprise the world with its power, it will crush its enemies.

CHAPTER TWENTY-TWO

FREEDOM OF SPEECH

The first amendment to the Constitution of the United States provides, among other things, that Congress shall make no law abridging the freedom of speech or of the press. But freedom of speech and freedom of the press are not rights which are absolute under all circumstances and conditions. What may have been freedom of speech yesterday may not be freedom of speech today. What may be freedom of speech in peace time may not be freedom of speech in time of war. Freedom is a relative term, and can mean no more than freedom regulated by just and impartial laws and not by arbitrary laws. Freedom of speech never meant unrestrained license to use an unbridled tongue. Under the Constitution of the United States, no one has a right to exercise his freedom of speech to the extent that it affects the safety or the general welfare of society.

We are living in perilous and dangerous days. The forms of government of many nations in the world are hostile, inimical, and antagonistic to our form of government, under the Constitution of the United States. Under our laws no one has a right to publish or communicate any teachings in sympathy with forms of government which are hostile, inimical or antagonistic to our form of government.

The time is here now, when those who think certain other forms of government are better than our own form of government, had better either get out and live under other forms of government, or get bridles for their tongues. This warning is not only intended for those who preach subversive doctrines in smoky, filthy, back rooms, but also for any of those who teach our youth in public schools, colleges, and universities, and who think the doctrines of the dictators are superior to the great principles laid down in the Constitution of the United States by our patriot forefathers. The people of this county will have no patience with any character of disloyalty in this hour. Disloyalty will be dealt with courageously, vigorously, and severely.

The late Justice Holmes, one of the greatest produced in the United States, who, in upholding the Espionage Act of the First World War, said:

"When a nation is at war, many things that might be said in time of peace are such a hindrance to its effort that their utterance will not be endured so long as men fight, and that no court could regard them as protected by any constitutional right."

CHAPTER TWENTY-THREE

GOLD STAR MOTHERS

We should not forget the soldier who made the supreme sacrifice by giving up his life for his country. He was only a boy; he had not yet become a man. He had a right to live and enjoy all of those things of life that countless millions before him had enjoyed.

We should also remember the one who went down into the valley of the shadow of death to give him life, —his mother. He began his existence with his mother. He was influenced by her from day to day. He grew and developed in the atmosphere she created. There he received his hurts and bruises and had them kissed away by her; there he learned to prattle, and then to talk; there he grew from babyhood to childhood; there he solved the mysteries about him one by one; there he grew from childhood into youth;—the land of dreams. His mother had seen the innocence of her babe; the blushes and fairness of her child; the brightness and energy of her boy.

She had a right to see him develop into maturity; to see his dreams come true; to walk with him along life's happy path. She had a right to his companionship during her declining years; and to his comfort and solace when her time came to drift across the river into the greatest of all adventures.

Her sacrifice is supreme, for she has given up that which is dearer to her than her own life,—her son.

CHAPTER TWENTY-FOUR

DISLOYALTY

For a century and a half this great country has been called a land of opportunity for the downtrodden of Europe. This country has been all of that and more. It has not only been a land of opportunity to the downtrodden; it has been a godsend and a blessing. It has not only fed the unfortunate; it has unlocked their energies. It has permitted them to express themselves; to worship as they please; and to assemble. It has given them a free mind and a free spirit.

There is some disloyalty to be found in this downtrodden group for which America has done so much. Some of them belong to subversive organizations which have aims that are hostile and inimical to our American ideals of government. There is no accurate way to explain them. They are impatient. They appear to be radicals who have no respect for the past. They are disgusted with the present. They see no good in society as it is now organized. Their aim is to revolutionize everything now, with violence or by any other means, regardless of the consequences, and create a "new order" in which they will be the chief actors.

No words can be found which so accurately describe their spirit and aims as the following words of Shakespeare:

> "Nay, had I power, I should
> Pour the sweet milk of concord into hell,
> Uproar the universal peace, confound
> All unity on earth."

CHAPTER TWENTY-FIVE

UNITY

If a nation has no mind, then it is a mere helpless mob. If it has two minds, it is weak. If it has several minds, it is confused and impotent. If it has one mind for wrong, it will eventually perish. If it has one mind for right, it is invincible; it will never pass away.

A nation does not necessarily become strong because of its numbers. It does not become strong because of the extent of its territory. The strength of a nation is in the character and unity of its people.

The individual may feel that he is insignificant and unimportant. He may feel that anything he thinks and says and does will not, in any way, affect the destiny of his country. If he will once realize that this country dwells in him, then he will immediately feel his responsibility and know that anything he thinks, or says or does vitally affects his country, either for its gain or for its loss.

The uninterrupted teamwork and constant cooperation of every living soul in preserving American institutions, traditions and principles will give the greatest strength to our nation.

PART V

CHILDREN

PART V

CHILDREN

CHAPTER TWENTY-SIX

A CHILD

The death of a little child is the greatest tragedy that can come to the world. Every child born into this world has a right to experience all the adventures of a good and useful life. It has a right to all the experiences of an exuberant childhood, and when the dawn of rosy childhood is past, it has a right to experience the dreams and feel the energy of youth; it has a right to feel the warmth of life's ascending sun, and to develop into maturity; it has a right to have its dreams come true, and to walk with love along life's happy path, and to hear the childish glee of a new generation; it has a right to feel the strength of life's noonday sun, and in that strength to accomplish the objects of its ambition here, and to feel that the world is a little better for its having lived; it has a right to slip into the evening time of life; and there in the quiet and peaceful breezes of life's descending sun, let the gracious boon of memory carry it back over the span of years

135

with all its soothing influences, comforting it with the thought of the adventures of that traveled road; and when that sun has set, it has a right to be surrounded by medical science and its loved ones, and to drift across the river as if in a fairy bark into that greatest of all adventures.

A child has a right to have conditions under which it lives and moves, reasonably safe.

CHAPTER TWENTY-SEVEN

AUTOMOBILES AND CHILDREN

Gentlemen, a child of tender years has just been killed in this county by a motor vehicle. I fear that many drivers of automobiles are not aware of the standard of care which they owe to a child of tender years who may be on or near the highway. The driver of an automobile owes not just ordinary care, but the highest degree of care toward a child of tender years who may be on or near the highway. A child in the public street or highway is not a trespasser. His right there is just as sacred as the driver of an automobile. A driver has no right to assume, under the law, that a child will manifest the judgment of an adult and must govern his conduct accordingly.

Children are capricious; they act heedlessly, without giving the slightest warning of their intention. They dart here and there with the superfluous energy of youth. It is true that streets and highways are not established for playgrounds, and this court is not encouraging such use of them; but children always have and always will put them to that use to some extent, and when children do this they do not, under the law, become trespassers. The driver of a motor vehicle is bound to know when he is driving on a busy street or highway that children are likely to be in the vicinity, and must act accordingly. He must drive at a rate of speed that will give him control of his car in an emergency. Drivers should remember that a child of tender years cannot, under the law, be negligent, and that even though the driver does all that is humanly possible after seeing the child in his pathway, that injury to the child may still be his fault, if he was in any manner careless immediately before seeing the child.

CHAPTER TWENTY-EIGHT

THE PHILOSOPHY OF HAPPINESS

The question involved here is the custody of two girls. This question comes up on a writ of habeas corpus. The father of the girls, filed his petition asking for the custody of his two daughters.

A voluminous amount of evidence has been taken. The evidence briefly shows that the father and mother of these girls separated about five years ago; that these girls lived with their grandmother; that their mother remained with the girls in the home of the grandmother; that she worked and helped to support her girls. The mother died May 8, 1934. Prior to the death of the mother, these two little girls had the care of a grandmother and a mother. Recently the grandmother died. Now the girls are left without the tender care of either. The one who now has the custody is not related to them.

These girls are now in or approaching the most critical and dangerous period of their lives. They need the attention that can only be given by the tender and loving hand of a woman. That they are not getting now.

What alternative does this court have before it?

The father is asking for the custody. Since the death of his wife, the father of the girls has remarried. His new wife has two children. She is not related to these children. There is enough evidence in this case to show that the father was not as good as he should have been. These girls unquestionably had a good mother. The father took the easy road. The father and mother had some difficulty. The evidence is not clear as to the cause. The court is of the opinion from the evidence that the fault was with the father. There are probably scores of husbands in this county today who have difficulty with their wives, but those same husbands are found at the old fireside keeping the family together, helping the mother train the children. They are there because they brought helpless children into the world, know they are needed, and will not turn their backs on the highest duty that can come to any man,—care for his own children. This father cannot be put in that class.

The letter from the mother presented in this case by the father will show that. That letter is worth reading:

"Monongalia County Hospital
"April 7, 1934

"I long ago decided never to ask a thing of you for myself and nothing for Jean and Doris as long as I was in condition to work for them. You know my health was ruined the first year we were married and had I had the operation Dr. Hunger said was necessary for me to be well, I would not be here today. I'm not sorry I worked for my little girls. I'm only glad I have been able to do for them what I have, but I'm asking you to carry on for them in case anything happens to me, care for and raise them the way I have in the past. And give them the education I had hopes of giving them and see that they are happy,—for I never knew happiness until the past seventeen months. And the greatest happiness was in being able to do for and making my girls happy and I know they have always been happy with me,—so if you are the man I thought you were a few years ago, you'll do your best for those little girls. Remember being happy is making someone else happy,—surely you can give up all long enough for them to grow up. God will do you justice whichever you do."

But this father is still their father. He has a father's heart. He will be given all the consideration by this court he deserves, and all that the law gives him under all the evidence in the case. The parents are the natural guardians of their children. Parents have a natural right to their offspring, unless they have entirely abandoned them. The evidence does not show that these children have been abandoned. The father has always manifested an interest in them,—not such an interest as he should have, but an interest.

The welfare of these two little girls,—sweet and intelligent,—is paramount to the claim of anyone else.

This court in deciding this case is interested only in the peace and happiness and safety and future of these two girls.

The paternal grandparents have attended every hearing in this case. They have manifested a natural interest in these girls,—the interest that grandparents usually manifest. The evidence shows that they have always helped support these girls. The grandmother is fifty-three years old and the grandfather is fifty-four years old. They both appear to be in good health. They are both intelligent. They both own considerable property. They live in a large and comfortable home. Their home is near that of the father. Their farms adjoin. The evidence is clear that the grandparents are good, reliable, sturdy, Christian folk. Their testimony reveals that they are very fond of Doris and Jean. They both testified that they would like to have the care and custody of these girls.

This court has decided to transfer their custody to their father, but they shall be maintained in the home of the grandfather and grandmother of these girls. There the court feels they will have the protective hand of a sturdy grandfather, and the loving care of a Christian grandmother. There they will be near their father, where he will have full opportunity to carry out the wishes of their deceased mother, expressed to him in a letter from her death bed in the hospital.

CHAPTER TWENTY-NINE

WELFARE OF CHILDREN

Gentlemen, I have spoken to you today, as judge of the criminal court. The judge of this circuit has many more duties. He is also the chancellor, civil judge, domestic relations judge and juvenile judge.

You have heard it said lately that juvenile delinquency is on the increase. That statement is generally true.

Recently Clay S. Crouse, the distinguished Judge of the Juvenile Court of Raleigh County, West Virginia, in discussing juvenile delinquency said:

"Today I would direct your attention to a salvage campaign in which we should all be more actively engaged—a campaign to salvage the youth of our land. Juvenile crime is on the increase throughout the nation and greatly on the increase in our own county. The juvenile courts are probably the greatest collectors of 'scrap' in all the land. Each day brings before the Juvenile Court a full quota of anti-social boys and girls accused of criminal offenses. It is the Judge of the Juvenile Court's grave responsibility to take this 'scrap' as he finds it, and then, by using all his patience and ingenuity, find out the reason for the delinquent's warped mental and moral attitude, and if possible, find something really fine and useful in the boy or girl before him, just as our Government today is turning what was one time considered useless ore, into shining, useful metal."

That is a good statement.

We are beginning to realize that the ultimate strength of a nation lies in its youth. The degree of that strength depends on the kind of men and women that nation develops. It is most essential in war time that we keep our boys and girls strong and healthy. We need the energy of our youth now. It is vital to the existence of this nation.

What are the causes of juvenile delinquency? Heredity, of course, has something to do with it. There are a few children who, unfortunately, are feeble-minded. A few have inherited some weakness. Some may have inherited some disease. Some may need medical attention. But environment is the chief cause of juvenile delinquency. Sometimes older boys lead younger ones astray. Sometimes adults contribute to their delinquency. In a large number of cases a child's delinquency is traced directly to his home life.

In most instances of juvenile delinquency one of the following conditions exist:

The parents are separated; or one parent is dead and the one left cannot take proper care of the children; or both parents are dead; or the parents quarrel and fight continuously; or one or both parents drink intoxicating liquors to excess; or one or both parents have some improper love affair; or the father is too busy with his work; or the mother is too busy with her social affairs to give the children proper attention, and to lead them in the paths of righteousness. Usually when a child becomes delinquent, it is either some adult's fault, or attributable to circumstances over which the child has no control.

Since I have been on this bench, I have sent only five boys to the Reform School at Pruntytown, and they were sent because there was nothing else to do, either because of the seriousness of the crime, or because there was no place else to send them. I have been criticized for not sending more.

Most boys who become delinquent are not really bad boys. They are unfortunate. They need help, guidance, and encouragement. There is seldom, if ever, a boy brought before me who is actually bad at heart.

No reform school is a good place for a child, if it can be avoided. "Reform School" is a misnomer. It doesn't usually reform.

No child should be sent to the reform school unless he has committed a serious crime, or unless he is naturally bad, or unless there is no other place to send the child.

In dealing with delinquent children since I have

been on the bench, I have not coddled them. I have put most of them on probation, with strict conditions to live up to for a definite period of time. More than ninety per cent of them have made good, have complied with the conditions, and have been dismissed with words of encouragement.

The best remedy for juvenile delinquency is to prevent it. It can be prevented in the following ways:

1. Good parents can prevent it by setting good examples, and by giving up many of their own desires, inclinations, and pleasures, in order to give their growing child the best possible attention.

2. Schools do much to keep the child on the right path. Very many delinquent children have either quit school, or are very irregular in attendance. Regular attendance in school is one of the surest safeguards against delinquency. No child should be allowed to be idle. Idleness leads children into trouble. Innocent play is not idleness.

3. In the summer when school is not in session, something must be substituted to take its place. A supervised playground does much to help the child. It keeps him busy. It keeps him in the open air and the sunshine. It gives him exercise and develops his body. It keeps him out of hideaway places, which are very bad for the child.

Society has a tremendous responsibility in providing recreation for the growing child. Adult society in many places in America has made a dismal failure in this respect. Almost all the money spent by society for recreation is spent for recreation for adults. Our lodges, clubs, civic organizations, golf courses and almost all other social organizations are for adults.

It is true children are on the golf course, but to carry the clubs of adults. Those who make moving pictures seldom make one for children. Adults do not demand it. Many communities spend one thousand dollars for adult recreation, while they spend one dollar for the recreation of children, and then wonder why they have so much juvenile delinquency. I am amazed that they do not have more.

Pick up your morning paper and see how many "ads" for rent read, "for adults only". These rent "ads" give us a fair example of the attitude of adults toward children today. Too many adults do not want to sacrifice for them. They do not want to be inconvenienced by them. But they want these children to fight for them and protect their investments and their hides the very minute they reach the age of eighteen.

Children in America should get a better "break" than they do.

4. Work does more to keep a child out of trouble than anything else. I do not mean hard work. A child in the city does not have the opportunity for work

the child on the farm has. He does not have the chance to bring in the cows, or to milk them, or to churn, or to cut stove wood, or to harness the horse, or to hoe corn, or to feed the chickens. But there are many things at which the child can be kept busy in the city. He can work on the lawn, in the garden, around the house. Parents should find something for the child to do that is useful.

If parents will see that their children attend school regularly, and that they are busy at useful work, or interesting and wholesome play, their children will never be in the juvenile court.

Not only parents, but society has a tremendous responsibility to the children of today. The children today will make America tomorrow. Their responsibilities may be heavier than ours. They deserve the best attention and all the training we can give them. The children of today are all right. My observation has been that they are better than their parents. I know of children who are providing for and taking care of younger brothers and sisters, and those who are doing this are still in their "teens", and this is being done in instances where the fathers and mothers are living, are not old, but are worthless.

When I was aspiring to the judgeship, I made a representation to the people of this county, and that representation was as follows:

"I am keenly interested in the welfare of the boys and girls, and I assure the fathers and mothers of Monongalia County that as Judge of the Circuit Court I will do everything possible for the protection of our children."

That I have done, and that I intend to continue to do.

The mistreating of a child is the most cowardly thing an adult can do. That child will never forget it, whether it is mistreated physically, or neglected, or led astray.

Delinquency among children can never be eliminated until we first eliminate delinquency of parents.

CHAPTER THIRTY

MY BEST FRIEND

The best man I have ever known intimately was an old farmer down in Ritchie County, West Virginia. He used to talk to me frequently when I was a boy. He gave me advice from time to time. He never told me what not to do; he told me what to do. He didn't drive me; he led me. I used to ride horseback with him and drive with him in the buggy. I worked with him on the farm. He talked to me a lot. He told me much about life that a boy my age should know.

I used to go out with him to feed the cattle and to take care of the sheep and lambs, when the snow was on the ground. After the chores were all done in the evening, he usually read. Often he read the Bible and explained it to me in front of the large open fireplace, while the wood crackled in front of the big backlog and the oil lamp stood on the table; and the big shepherd dog lay in front of the fire with his head between his paws, contented because of a day's work well done, after he had brought in the cows and rounded up the sheep. This man's devoted wife sat there busy with her knitting, if her work was all done in the kitchen.

He died when I was fifteen years old. He left this

earth when I was a mere boy, but his work was done as far as I was concerned. He had trained me. He taught me things that no one else could have taught me. He had left me something that money could not have bought. He was the best friend I have ever had. He was my father.

Every father should be his child's best friend. A father does not have to be rich; it is not necessary for him to be a college graduate to be the best friend his child will ever have. All he needs is character, a realization of his importance to his child and a willingness to sacrifice some of his time from day to day to train him.

Too many fathers miss a golden opportunity to train their children when they are young; to teach them the simple things of life; and to lead them in the paths of righteousness and in the way they should go. If every father will leave his child this heritage, the problem of juvenile delinquency will disappear. This heritage is far more important than for his child to inherit fabulous wealth.

PART VI

THE DEVELOPMENT OF LAW AND ITS IMPORTANCE

PART VI

THE DEVELOPMENT OF LAW AND
ITS IMPORTANCE

CHAPTER THIRTY-ONE

THE TEMPLE OF JUSTICE

In this Temple of Justice, tragedy often stalks; demons of revenge lie in wait; despair at times reigns supreme; distressing cries of regret are heard; here float the dark clouds of gloom; hearts come here upon which has fallen the darkness of night; human beings enter this Temple, upon whose brows are carved scenes of shame and disgrace.

But on the other hand, tragedy often surrenders to delight and joy; those who come with savage cries for vengeance often leave with hearts that lovingly forgive; despair sees the fickle star of hope; intermingled with cries of regret are heard soft words of forgiveness; here, the thorns of hatred mingle with the flowers of love; and above all, in this Temple where are registered all the emotions of human life, there are always hovering near, the angels of mercy and justice.

CHAPTER THIRTY-TWO

AMERICAN JUSTICE

This court has found these indictments involving Communist Activities insufficient to charge a crime, under our laws. But if what these indictments allege is true, some of you are reprehensible. You do not deserve American justice.

This great nation has been good to the world, and particularly to Europe. In the past we not only opened our doors to overcrowded Europe, but in 1917 and 1918 we sent two million American boys over there,— two million of the greatest fighting hearts the world had ever seen. We sent two million soldiers to Europe to free it from the same tyranny that is now enveloping it.

You people probably think the judge of this court is kind to you in quashing these indictments. You are wrong if you do. The judge of this court has not been kind to you; American justice has been kind to you. American justice will not lower its standards to punish even those who appear to be hostile to American ideals. You are fortunate that you are being judged under the standards and principles of American justice. Personally, I do not think you deserve what you are getting. I think a lot of trash should be cleaned out of this country.

CHAPTER THIRTY-THREE

JUDICIAL TEMPERAMENT

Laymen and lawyers alike talk loosely about judicial temperament, without realizing what it is. It is my belief that it consists of the following fundamental elements.

The first is courage. It is my opinion that no requirement is more important than the requirement of courage, particularly in this judicial circuit during the next eight years.

This circuit during the next eight years will be no place for a hothouse plant; it will be no place for one who has been sheltered through life. It will require one, who, like a sturdy tree in the open, has been exposed to the storms of life. A man without stamina will be out of place as judge of this circuit.

The second requirement is intellectual honesty. The lack of this kind of honesty is covered by the Commandment "Thou shalt not steal", but some people fail to recognize this fact. Intellectual honesty, or the lack of it, is more subtle than common honesty, or the lack of it. No man is qualified for the judgeship who is not intellectually honest. The mind of a judge must go straight. It must not permit the slighting or warping of facts for the purpose of changing the result of a decision. The ancient and noble profession of horse trading is all right, but it has no place on the bench.

The third requirement is a broad background of experience in human affairs. Law is as broad as the experience of the human race. The wider a man's experience has been through life, the better opportunity he has to make a good judge. If a judge does not know the law at the moment, as applied to a case that may be before him, he can find it in the books; but he cannot find experience which he may lack. Experience is acquired over the years. Experience which fits a man for the judgeship does not come from a life of ease, but from a life of struggle and strenuous endeavor.

The fourth requirement is common sense, combined with a sense of fairness. We do not acquire common sense; we either have it or we do not. We acquire knowledge, but knowledge without common sense is folly; with common sense it is wisdom. An old Persian proverb says, one pound of knowledge requires ten pounds of common sense to apply it. A lawyer may know more about the law books than any of his associates at the bar; but if he lacks the degree of common sense necessary to apply his knowledge, then he is disqualified for the judgeship.

A sense of fairness means that the judge must close every avenue to self-interest, vanity, self-conceit, obstinacy, and prejudice; and that I will do.

The fifth is a knowledge of the law, and the ability to take a new set of facts and arrive at justice. Aristotle says justice is to give every man his own. That will be my constant aim. To be perfectly just is not an attribute of man; it is an attribute of the Divine. I will be just to the utmost of my abilities. I can do no more.

CHAPTER THIRTY-FOUR

A QUASI-JUDICIAL OFFICER

Mr. Prosecutor, I want to congratulate you for frankly stating that you do not believe you have made a case. I am of the same opinion, and I am also glad that you are honest enough and fair enough to see both sides of a case. It is true that the prosecuting attorney cannot possibly see all the evidence on both sides of a case until it is produced. I think that the State has failed to make a case here, through no fault on the part of the prosecuting attorney.

The prosecuting attorney is a quasi-judicial officer, and it is his duty to prosecute with all the vigor that he can. We have lawyers on both sides. It is the duty of the prosecuting attorney to represent the State; but when he comes to the close of the trial where he sees clearly that he has not made a case against the defendant, beyond a reasonable doubt, then it is his duty to say so.

Too many prosecutors just try to make a record. They get too much like the hunter. They want to see how many people they can convict.

The prosecuting attorney should use all of his ability and energy to get all the evidence possible and to convict anybody he honestly believes is guilty; but when he comes to a place in a case where he feels in his heart, after the evidence has developed, that the man is not guilty, then it is his duty to say so. But it takes courage to do this. The motion to dismiss is granted. The record may show that one juror is withdrawn, and a verdict is directed in favor of the defendant.

CHAPTER THIRTY-FIVE

HOW LONG IS THE ARM OF THE COURT?

A short time ago the editor of one of the news-papers here very properly asked in an editorial how long the arm of the court was. The arm of this court, under the law in this State, is long enough to reach to the home of any juror, witness, or party to a suit, and protect him from any violence or threats of violence, while he is traveling to the court, or returning home from the court. This court brings witnesses into this court. Many of them come against their will, and testify reluctantly. Many witnesses dislike to become involved in litigation. This court under the law can protect them, and will protect them. But this court, also, from now on will expect, demand, and see, as far as it is within the power of the court, that all wit-nesses tell the truth.

This court will also protect those who testify from this witness stand while in the presence of the court. Cross-examination of a witness by an attorney is the best method we have devised for ascertaining, not just the truth, but the whole truth. Witnesses must submit to a proper cross-examination. They must be willing to have the searchlight turned on them. But this court will not permit any witness to be improperly ques-tioned, or to be slandered.

CHAPTER THIRTY-SIX

PERJURY

Recently, J. Edgar Hoover, Chief of the Federal Bureau of Investigation, made the following statement: "We have today in the courts of our country the most appalling scourge of perjury ever known in the history of America." That statement is probably true. After watching witnesses from this bench, I have come to the conclusion that many of them have not told the truth.

To swear falsely on the witness stand is more serious than most people realize. In the first place, it is contrary to all the teachings of the human race. In the 20th verse of the Fifth Chapter of Deuteronomy we find the Commandment: "Neither shalt thou bear false witness against thy neighbor." In the 9th verse of the Nineteenth Chapter of Proverbs we find the statement: "A false witness shall not be unpunished; and he that speaketh lies shall perish." In the 5th verse of the Third Chapter of Malachi we find a warning against "false swearers", and in the 10th verse of the First Chapter of Timothy we find that those who perjure themselves are classed with the ungodly and lawless.

The teachings we find in the Bible are not the law

which this court must follow. But when I study those teachings carefully, I find that the law in West Virginia is probably based on those teachings.

The law in West Virginia is that a person convicted of perjury may be confined in the State Penitentiary for as long as ten years; and that is not all of the punishment. The interesting part of that statute is that the latter part of it reads like the Bible. That part provides that any person convicted of perjury shall be adjudged forever incapable of holding any office of honor, trust or profit in this state, or of serving as a juror.

CHAPTER THIRTY-SEVEN

A DEFENDANT IS SURROUNDED BY EVERY SAFEGUARD

You have been given a fair trial. This court was most fair with you. Every instruction in your favor which your attorney asked for was given to the jury. The jury was instructed that they must presume you innocent until the State proved you guilty beyond a reasonable doubt. Your attorney put your character in issue and showed your good character. The State failed to rebut this. This court instructed the jury that since the State failed to rebut this evidence of good character, there was a presumption that the State was unable to do so. This court was liberal in allowing evidence in your favor.

But after all of this, a jury of twelve men, your neighbors and good citizens of this county, found you guilty of driving an automobile drunk on the public highway.

Many people today do not fully appreciate the fairness which is extended to all those in America who are accused of crime. First, one accused of crime must be indicted by a grand jury, which is made up of sixteen citizens from his county, twelve of whom must vote in favor of the indictment. Then the accused is tried before twelve men, all of whom must agree that the accused has been proved guilty beyond a reasonable doubt. You will recall that the jury was polled in your case and that each juror was asked if a verdict of "guilty" was his verdict, and each juror answered in the affirmative.

It has been the unpleasant opportunity of the judge of this court to see many American citizens tried for offenses, when they were deprived of the right of trial by jury; deprived of the right to be represented by an attorney; deprived of all the safeguards set up around one accused of crime in this country. Those American citizens were soldiers in the American Army in a foreign country, and were tried before a court martial officer. Their trials were brief. I saw one American soldier, tried, sentenced to death, and executed,—all on the same day. That was war. But in this country today through reckless and drunken driving, as many Americans are being killed each year as were killed in World War I in the same length of time. This slaughter must stop.

Until you appeared in this Court with this crime, the judge of this court was not acquainted with you; but if my best friend stood there in your shoes today, the judge of this court would have no right to shirk his duty. It is not pleasant to sentence you to jail; and if my best friend stood there convicted as you are of the crime of driving drunk, although my heart would bleed, it would be my duty to sentence him. And if he was the kind of a man we all think our best friends are, he would go like a man, realizing that it is the duty of the judge of a court to always do the right thing, as far as he is able to see the right, and not to respect persons. He would go like a man, realizing that his going to jail for driving drunk may save many a loving mother in this county the awful anguish of some day looking down at the mangled form of that which means more to her than her own life,—her little child.

CHAPTER THIRTY-EIGHT

THE LAW MUST APPLY EQUALLY

The law must apply equally to everyone. The law must not be partial. There must not be one law for some and another law for others. Dictatorship is based on personalities. Democracy is based on the law. The quickest way to undermine a democracy is to administer the law unequally. We are all equal before the law.

CHAPTER THIRTY-NINE

WE MUST DEPEND ON LAW

In dictator countries, armies and gestapos are formed to keep the people in order. But in a democracy, such as ours, we must depend on the law.

Each citizen must be protected in his property, reputation, liberty, and life. This can only be done by firmly and justly administrating the law. The law must never be relaxed. The home front must be kept in order while the boys fight on the battlefronts. No man must be permitted to even think that he is bigger than the law. No man must ever be allowed to take the law into his own hands.

CHAPTER FORTY

A GOVERNMENT OF LAWS

Society is always tottering. It is always in a very delicate state of balance. It is always threatened. It is never at rest. It lives in the midst of snares. Law is the only force that guarantees security to society. It is the only force that can protect society from itself. It is the only force in this country which prevents any man from assuming dictatorial powers, for this is a government of laws, and not a government of men.

The rights of the people in America are not determined by the opinions, whims, prejudices, tastes, personal feelings, or desires of men who hold office, or by any other set of men; those rights have been established by a set of laws which were in process of development long before the Barons wrested the Magna Charta from King John at Runnymede.

Americans obey no master but the law. No one is above the law. Everyone, regardless of his position in life, is subordinate to the law. We do not have in America a select few who can do no wrong. The law is strong enough in America to prevent any set of men from making the people mere puppets and slaves.

CHAPTER FORTY-ONE

THE COMMON LAW

The common law was not born in a day. Principles of law which we use today, like the pebbles that are thrown upon the beach, have been fashioned during the ages. When a court decides a case on its merits, the decision not only determines the rights of the parties in that particular case, but it also settles the principles involved in it as permanent rules of law, applicable in all future cases embracing similar facts and involving the same principles.

The decision of a court becomes public law; it measures private rights and determines the status of property. We call this common law. This is sometimes improperly referred to as judge-made law. It is not judge-made law, but it is that law which our judges discover from time to time. It always existed, but it was not discovered until some judge rendered his decision. The common law has been discovered and built up by long-continued and arduous labors. It is interwoven with the interests, the experiences, the habits, the sentiments, the hopes and aspirations of our people. It has grown with our growth and expanded with our experience, until it has ripened into the common law of today.

The common law is one of the strong pillars on which American democracy rests.

CHAPTER FORTY-TWO

THE DEVELOPMENT OF LAW

The most learned jurists find themselves at a loss to define the term "law". Long before there were courts, there was a great body of law that a man was bound not to violate and that was generally obeyed.

When we think of man from a physical standpoint, we must think of him as being about the same as in the beginning. The laws which govern his birth, his growth, his decay, and his death are the same. Human effort has failed to change them.

The ant is law-abiding, because it is governed solely by instinct, and has no power to change. The ant is no wiser than it was a million years ago. It has no intelligence. It is governed by a natural law, just the same as the moon, or the stars. But this is not true of man. Man has done something no other creature on this earth has been able to do. Man has become independent. He has acquired a free will. His mind has been developing through the ages. This development is very slow. Man has passed from that state of primitive man, where he was wholly obedient to his circumstances and surroundings, into a free world of thought and a world of dreams.

Man will probably never have a perfect society like the ant. Man will probably never be perfectly law-abiding, because he has a free will; but the highest type of man is the one who recognizes his duty to obey the laws. Man is controlled by both his instincts and his intelligence. He has acquired the power of reasoning. While man has a reasoning mind, he still carries with him the instincts of the primitive man, such as anger, greed, envy, covetousness, selfishness and lust. The difference between men today is that about ninety-five per cent of the people of this country today have intellects and moral sentiments, which command and control these instincts, and the other five per cent do not have such intellects and moral sentiments.

Countless ages ago, man,—a poor, naked, helpless wretch, started on his conquest of the world. All he had was his instincts and a larger brain than anything else on this earth. We learn in the 3rd Chapter of Genesis that man knew not good and evil. To put it another way, in the beginning man did not know the difference between right and wrong. It is to the eternal credit of man that he has lifted himself to his present state. His original mind which did not know good from evil has developed into a reasoning mind; but he has trailing along with all of this development his old original instincts. These old instincts which man today carries with him, as a burden, and which down through the ages he has been unable to entirely cast aside, are the reason for this grand jury here today.

The earliest man gave us the basis for all law. He learned to act in such a way that he would not endanger the social existence of the community. The result was that all men had a tendency to act alike. They had no ruler, no king, no judge. None was necessary with the earliest man. He was governed by the opinion of all the community. If he acted different from the other members, he was driven out, and like the drone ants, he would accept death, rather than leave, for he had no place to go. Thus we see the earliest man gave us the foundation for our law today, because he tried to please those with whom he came in daily contact. He was governed solely by the opinion of the whole community. Today we have voluntary blackouts. When a man refuses to turn his lights out, he shows himself to be less obedient to the opinion of the community than the primitive man.

Men finally developed a spoken language, and by means of this spoken language began to learn something about the minds of the others, and began to get some glimmerings of a personality. Men began to be conscious of themselves. This consciousness of self is the basis for what we call "conscience" today. As soon as man developed a conscience, he began to have moral sentiments. Law has developed as the moral sentiments of the community have developed. The law for the primitive man was simply the customs which had been acted upon for ages. The primitive man was unconsciously doing what seemed to him to be right.

The primitive man was not capable of thinking in terms of the individual. All relatives were responsible to another tribe for what one of their own members did. What Hitler does repeatedly in punishing a whole community or a whole race for what one member of that community or race has done, takes him back at least a hundred thousand years to primitive man.

We see that the early man gave us the raw materials on which all criminal law is based today. Some of these raw materials are: a desire to please those with whom we come in contact; moral sentiments; every man has a right to act as others act; social instincts; and a crude sense of justice, which the Old Testament expresses as "an eye for an eye and a tooth for a tooth".

The only peoples of importance in the development of law belong to the Caucasian race, and we belong to the Aryan branch of that race. We find that among the Aryans, the only method of redress for violations of the customary laws, resulting in injury to others, was what we call self-help, backed by public opinion, and by making the kindred of the injurer responsible as a whole to the kindred of the injured. The individual was helpless. This primitive Aryan was still unable to comprehend the conception of an individual.

A history of the law of civilized men begins with the Semites, a branch of the Caucasian race, in Babylonia. From there it passed to Palestine, then to the Greeks, to the Romans, to Continental Europe, to the English, and to America.

The oldest collection of laws in existence is the Code of King Hammurabi. It dates back to 2250 years before Christ. This code was the old, settled customs of primitive man reduced to writing.

But what we call crime today was still a private offense. The individual still was helpless and counted for nothing.

We now pass to the Hebrew Law, the law as set forth in the Bible. The Hebrew tribes had a patriarchal form of family and a tribal organization. We see Moses a very busy man, wearing himself out, sitting as judge of all the disputes of the people. Jethro, the father-in-law of Moses, was the first reformer of legal procedure. In the 18th Chapter of Exodus, we learn that one day Jethro went to watch Moses sitting as judge. Jethro said in substance; Moses, the thing that thou doest is not good. You are working too hard. You are wearing yourself out. You ought to hear only the important cases, and appoint other men to hear the little disputes. Moses followed Jethro's advice, and that was the beginning of our system of courts.

Before the Hebrew Law, an innocent child could be put to death for his father's wrong, or a mother could be put to death for a son's wrong. The greatest and most distinct triumph of the Hebrew Law is the recognition of the individual. We find in the Bible, in the 16th Verse of the 24th Chapter of Deuteronomy, the following statement: "The fathers shall not be put to death for the children; neither shall the children be put to death for the fathers. Every man shall be put to death for his own sin."

This means that with the Hebrew Law, human beings have finally come to the place in the development of the law where the individual is responsible only for his own acts, and not for the acts of some other individual, because the other happens to belong to the same family or tribe. This was one of the greatest steps in the development of the law, because it recognized the individual as having rights of his own. When the individual was recognized, the history of liberty began. Man took on a new personality. He began to think for himself. The progress of the human race went forward with increased speed.

The Romans had a criminal court; they recognized public wrongs; they recognized the individual; they established competent tribunals. They were the first to develop a profession of lawyers.

While the Roman law recognized individual personality, recognized that the individual had rights, the individual was not protected from the State. No man was safe from the attacks of the informer or demagogue. No man in the Roman Empire was safe from persecution, because they had not yet conceived the idea of a tribunal such as this grand jury chosen from the people to determine what individuals should be prosecuted.

We pass now into the Dark Ages. The Roman Empire fell to pieces. The German barbarian of the North destroyed the costly fabric of civilization. All laws were unsettled and in confusion. The church kept alive some parts of the Roman law, but profound lawyers had left the earth. During the Dark Ages men had become ignorant, degraded and superstitious; but even then the sentiment for law and justice had become so ingrained in the human race, that there was a constant demand made all through these Dark Ages for a reign of law.

After the German barbarians in the Dark Ages had destroyed all governmental institutions and reduced the civilized world to chaos, England became the chosen home of legal development under the Norman race with its genius for law. Up to this time the world had never had a grand jury. The human race had never conceived the idea of having a cross section of the people themselves determine what individuals should be tried for committing a wrong. Before the origin of the grand jury, the people of England were many times persecuted in the name of the Crown. Since the existence of the grand jury, it has stood as a barrier against any persecution of the people. The grand jury was England's greatest legal contribution to the United States. The institution we call the grand jury has been safely tucked away in the Constitution of the United States, and cannot be destroyed, except by a vote of the people.

PART VII

THE SECURITY OF AMERICA

PART VII

THE SECURITY OF AMERICA

CHAPTER FORTY-THREE

TOLERANCE

When I was a boy growing up, my father used to call me in the middle of the night and say, "The woods are afire again." And I remember how I would jump out of bed and go out into the darkness, and over the hills and through the woods to the scene of the fire. What were we going for? To save the old rail fence. We would rake a wide path between that old rail fence and that raging fire, and then fire against it. When our fire met that raging fire, it made no struggle; it flickered for a moment and disappeared. In every generation, the fires of bigotry and intolerance rage for a while in this country, like great forest fires. When these fires come, we must backfire on them. We must turn the fire of truth toward them and meet them half way. When this back fire meets these raging fires of bigotry and intolerance, they will make no struggle; they will flicker for a moment and disappear.

A man came into my office a few days ago on bus-

183

iness. When he was through his business and started
to leave, he said, "Are you supporting Mr. Blank?" I
said, "I am." I then asked him if he intended to vote
for him. He said that he certainly did not, and added
that he didn't see how any good conscientious Protestant American could "stomach" him. I said, "Sit
down; I want to ask you a question. Why did you use
the word, 'Protestant;' what does that have to do with
choosing a public official?" He replied, "Well, he is
a Catholic." I said, "What does that have to do with
it?" He hesitated. Then I inquired, "Just why are you
against him?" He responded, "I am against him because he is a Catholic." I said, "Do you know that you
are a bad American citizen?" He got red in the face.
I continued, "I want to go a little further. You are
a nullifier of the Constitution of the United States."
He got redder in the face. I said, "I will go further.
You are a vandal." He jumped up and out of his chair.
I said, "Wait a minute; sit down. I will defend myself
with the Constitution of the United States." I turned
to Article VI of the Constitution, which says, "no religious test shall ever be required as a qualification to
any office or public trust under the United States."
I said, "If there are enough vandals in this country
who vote against this candidate, simply because of his
religion, to defeat him on Election Day, then the next
day after election you and the rest of the vandals

should be compelled to walk to Monticello, the resting place of Thomas Jefferson, and tear from his tomb his own epitaph." What was that epitaph? When Thomas Jefferson felt himself nearing the time when he must pass to the great beyond, he wrote his own epitaph. He mentioned nothing about being Governor of Virginia; he mentioned nothing about being Ambassador to France; he mentioned nothing about being Vice-President of the United States; he mentioned nothing about serving two terms as President of the United States. But he wrote, "Thomas Jefferson, Author of the Declaration of Independence. Founder of the University of Virginia. And author of the Virginia Statute of Religious Freedom." The Constitution of West Virginia has embodied this statute, and every state in the Union has followed the Virginia example.

Protestants cannot take advantage of religious liberty and deny it to others. There is an old maxim which says: "He is only free who lives among free men." We can no more be half free and half slave today, than when Lincoln said that this nation cannot endure half free and half slave.

This nation is tolerant. Its tolerance is one of its assets; it is one of its elements of strength.

CHAPTER FORTY-FOUR

THE SIXTH COLUMN

We have all heard much talk about the fifth column, which is composed of spies, traitors, secret agents, and saboteurs. But there is another column in the United States which must also be dealt with. I choose to call it the "sixth column". The "sixth column" is composed of the following groups of people in the United States:

It has in its ranks those who are slumbering; those who are not alert. Those who make up this group are careless about what they say; what they listen to; and what they believe. Many of them listen to members of the fifth column.

The psalmist said, "He that keepeth Israel shall neither slumber nor sleep." How true that is of America today. Those who keep America will not keep it long, if they are slumbering.

The "sixth column" has in its ranks that small group who lack courage; who, like some sheep, invite trouble by running away from it; or who like other sheep stand still, in a tremble, until the dogs are on them. They are the "peace at any price" class. They are the slackers.

The "sixth column" is composed also of that group who believe that in some mysterious way the Lord will take care of America; that somehow everything will come around all right. That group should remember that the Lord does not help those who do not try to help themselves. Our forefathers placed a firm reliance on the protection of Divine Providence; but at the same time they mutually pledged to each other their lives, their fortunes, and their sacred honor. Our forefathers did this at a time when they had to make that pledge good. We are not worthy of our heritage, unless we are willing to do the same thing.

The "sixth column" has in its ranks those who foolishly put themselves above their country. Their thoughts are colored either by envy, prejudice, greed, self-interest or political influence. They are willing for the youth of the nation to pay in blood for their protection; but they hate to pay in money or in inconvenience, or in social or political prestige. They love to wear the cloak of citizenship of the greatest nation in the world; but they hate to assume all the responsibilities of that citizenship.

The "sixth column" has that large group in its ranks who depend on the protection of two vast oceans, and who fail to realize that distance and space are being rapidly eliminated.

Those who depend on the protection of the oceans

from now on will be sadly disappointed, for the oceans have already been crossed by the fifth column. The parachute troops are already here. They will not drop from the skies. They will suddenly appear, seemingly from nowhere, like seventeen-year locusts, trained and ready to dynamite bridges, derail trains; blow up industrial plants and ammunition plants; destroy our communications; poison our food and water supplies; burn our materials; and engage in strategic sabotage activities in general, unless they are detected and destroyed before hostilities begin. They will carry on that kind of war they have learned from the teachings of General Ludendorff; that kind of war which undermines the enemy from within; that kind which sends bombing squadrons against civilians; that kind which is prepared behind the enemy's lines before hostilities begin. The totalitarian powers have undoubtedly plotted their course in this country. The fate of other countries is a grim warning to us.

In the "sixth column" is also found those who never see any danger of an invasion of the United States. Those who are found in this class should study a globe of the world. They will find that Iceland is only 850 miles from Norway, and much closer to Scotland; that Greenland is only 130 miles west of Iceland. They will find that Greenland is definitely in the Western Hemisphere; that it almost touches Canada; that it has a low-lying fringe of meadows; and that it has an area larger than England which is free from snow in the summer.

Is there any danger of an invasion of this country? Suppose the British fleet is captured or destroyed, and the totalitarian countries strike us simultaneously,— from the West and from the East,—then I repeat, is there any danger of an invasion while we are in our present state of preparedness?

Not so many weeks ago the people of this country were agitated concerning the possibility of sending an American Army to fight on foreign soil. That is no longer the paramount question before us. The question before us now is,—are we prepared to keep a foreign army from landing in the Western Hemisphere?

In the "sixth column" we also find those in our generation today who are sapping their vigor and strength, by dissipation and dishonorable diseases. I am firmly convinced that this element in the French population had more to do with their defeat than the fifth column, or powerful German tanks. The French had become weak and soft by riotous and immoral living.

We cannot prepare for the defense of this nation by the use of money alone. We have a large per cent of the gold in the world; but gold alone does not make us strong. In the last analysis, our strength depends on the character of our people.

This nation has now arrived at the place in its history, where in order to survive and endure, it must turn all of its able-bodied citizens, both male and female, away from the paths of ignoble ease, foolish pleasure and senseless dissipation; and put them on the broad highway of work, training, discipline and strenuous endeavor.

And finally, the "sixth column" is also composed of those who are gullible enough to believe that all those who preach peace are good Americans, and have the best interest of America at heart. They fail to recognize that many of those who preach peace are foreign propagandists. Many Americans have been listening to and repeating the propaganda songs of the totalitarian countries. Their secret agents have been singing their subtle songs into our ears, imploring us to follow the ways of peace. This nation does not need their advice. We are a peaceful people, but we do not want the kind of peace the totalitarian states would impose on us, if they had a chance.

We want peace, but we intend to have a peace of our own choosing,—an American peace, not a totalitarian peace.

The only way we can have an American peace is to be prepared to fight for it, if necessary, and to fight victoriously.

For a long time I have heard Americans say that

America's participation in the World War was a mistake. I have not shared in that sentiment. No one can say what the result would have been, if America had followed a cloistered life and remained indifferent as to what went on around it at the time of the World War. We do know that the liberty of the world was saved for twenty years. Wendell Willkie, not only the distinguished Republican nominee for President of the United States in 1940, who received twenty-two million American votes, but also a World War veteran, says in referring to our part in the World War: "The mistake we made was not that we fought then, but that we did not fight later to transform our victory into its full significance and possibilities."

We do know that two million American youth crossed an ocean three thousand miles wide, filled with dangerous submarines; that they landed in a strange country; hurled the Kaiser's best troops back from the Marne; and drove his forces of tyranny back through the forests of the Argonne.

I do not believe that the greatest of all crusades was in vain. There the soul of America shone forth in all its glory. There the greatest fighting hearts in all history flashed across the battlefields of France. There the warmest patriotic blood of all time gave unselfishly for the liberty of others.

The American youth who died in that world

struggle are immortal, for countless generations will draw strength from that reservoir of wealth left by them,—that reservoir filled with the spirit of human liberty, the emotions of courage, the examples of unselfishness, the pride of honor and the exemplification of all that is great and good in the American. Died in vain? No good American will defame their memory by saying so, for this nation will be nourished during the dark night that is now descending over it, on the legacy they left us.

I fear that hosts of Americans have been lulled to sleep by members of the fifth column, and that they are still in the arms of Morpheus, while the world blows up on all sides of them. I fear that many Americans have been unwittingly saying what Berlin wanted them to say.

We are in danger in this country today from the "sixth column", as well as from the fifth column. The "sixth columnists" have always existed. They existed in 1775, when Patrick Henry delivered his famous "Liberty or Death" speech; when he said, "Shall we gather strength by irresolution or inaction? Shall we acquire the means of effectual resistance by lying supinely on our backs, and hugging the delusive phantom of hope, until our enemies have bound us hand and foot?" They existed when Hitler wrote his *Mein Kampf*, and told the world what he intended to do;

when Hitler marched into the Rhineland in 1935;
when Hitler was permitted to rearm and to build the
West Wall; when Hitler marched into Austria,
Czecho-Slovakia, and Poland; when Hitler landed his
troops in Norway. Even after the invasion of Nor-
way, the "sixth columnists" were still in control of
England, led by the great appeaser,—Prime Minister
Chamberlain.

The "sixth columnists" are speaking up now in
America. One of the most distinguished of them
says, "No one wishes to attack us, and no one is in a
position to do so." Who gave him that astounding information? Does he claim to know the mind of Hitler? Suppose Hitler told him he did not wish to attack
us. He told Holland and Belgium the same thing. He
is very soothing and reassuring; so was Chamberlain.

This same distinguished gentleman also appears to
advise this nation to be ready to cooperate with Hitler
after the present war in Europe is over. He seems to
assume that Hitler will be the victor. For this nation
to be ready to cooperate with Hitler when the war is
over, amounts to cooperation now. This nation cannot, in any way, aid Hitler in his destruction of other
nations, and be true to the principles on which it is
based.

Members of the "sixth column" are not consciously
disloyal. They believe in their hearts, that they are

good Americans. But as "sixth columnists", they must be eliminated, not by force or violence; but by the warm sunshine of truth and public sentiment. When this is accomplished, then the people of this nation will be in a position, not only to successfully and completely destroy the fifth column, but to prepare this great nation to defeat decisively the other four columns any nation, or combination of nations, may send against us.

This nation must not begin the policy of appeasement toward any other nation. If we ever start that policy, we are lost. "Never carry gifts to your enemies," is a saying which is just as full of truth for nations as for individuals. This nation has never had any appeasement in its make-up; it has never retreated; it has always fought for its ideals. It must not, and will not, change the course of its history now.

I know what war is, but I do not fear war. What I fear is peace,—that kind of peace that Czecho-Slovakia, Poland, Norway, Denmark, Holland, Belgium, France, Yugoslavia and Greece in rapid succession, got, at the hands of a ruthless dictator; because they either were not able to resist at all, or were not able to resist successfully.

It is that kind of peace that America must prepare to avoid. That is the kind of peace we get at the price of liberty, honor and self-respect; at the price of tolerance, the Christian Cross, and democracy; at the price of free minds and free spirits; at the price of all the sublime sentiments and ideals of life which were made possible for us with the blood and the sweat and the tears of generations who resisted tyrants for the right to live.

The peace of death is far better than the peace of living, without those things of life which make it worth while to live.

CHAPTER FORTY-FIVE

A VICTORIOUS PEACE

I am firmly and definitely convinced that while we
are fighting this war and thinking and praying for a
victory on the battlefield, we must also be doing some
serious and straight thinking about the kind of peace
we will get. After we gain a victory on the battlefield,
it will be nullified if we fail to make a victorious peace.
Both victories are so closely tied together that we are
compelled to think about both at the same time. During the First World War the people at home thought
only of a military victory and were not prepared for
the peace which came. We must be prepared this time.

There is now high hope for a lasting peace because
the American people are beginning to realize that
peace cannot be had by simply wishing for it, by ig-
noring facts and history, by disarmament conferences,
by foolish neutrality laws and by silly isolation talk.

There are four ways by which we may get a victorious peace, after we have crushed Germany and Japan
on the battlefield:

The first is to keep absolute control of both Germany and Japan. We must disarm them completely.
We must take all their weapons away from them and

see that they do not make any more. They must be
policed by a large army of occupation. We should
provide against their organizing any spy system in
other countries. They must be taught that they are
not superior races. Let them know absolutely who
their masters are. They will respect us more for that
than if we show too much kindness and extend favors.
It is their nature to accept kindness as a sign of weakness. They do not understand generosity. They only
understand power, authority, orders and commands.
Both nations have demonstrated that they are not fit
to govern themselves, and, therefore, they must be
controlled.

The second way to get a victorious peace is to col-
laborate with the great powers and to have a definite
understanding with them. After this war is over, there
will be only three great powers, namely, the United
States, Great Britain, and Russia. If a common danger
has made it necessary for these great powers to unite
in war against that danger, why is it not good sense for
these great powers to remain united after the danger
has been averted, to prevent that danger or a similar
one from recurring. China will not be a great power
for some time to come because she does not have the
means of making the tools of war. But we should continue to cultivate the friendship of China.

The third way to get a victorious peace is to cooperate in some world organization that includes all nations except Germany and Japan.

The fourth way to get a victorious peace is to be prepared for war in peace time. We must not forget this time. We must not fall back into a false sense of security again. We have "got away" with that mistake for the last time. We must remember that the oceans which have protected us are rapidly becoming ponds, and that the air over us is a world highway. If Russia should fail to cooperate in a world organization, then we must build a more powerful military machine.

In making the peace, it is imperative that we aim at one thing, and that is security for this nation. That must be our primary aim. That must be our ultimate aim. We want peace, but we do not want peace without security. If there is any question between peace and security, we must choose security. In the making of the peace, security is the ball the American people must keep their eyes on.

CHAPTER FORTY-SIX

AMERICA MUST HAVE A CHRISTIAN SOUL

The first Amendment to the Constitution of the United States provided that, "Congress shall make no law respecting an establishment of religion, or prohibiting the free exercise thereof." That amendment made freedom of worship a part of the fundamental law of the land. That amendment put the right of a man to worship his God according to the dictates of his own conscience, beyond the control of any man or any set of men, for that right was safely tucked away in the Constitution. Christianity is not only one of the cornerstones of this nation; it is also one of the outstanding elements in giving this nation strength, stability and security.

But I am convinced that before this nation can become what we desire, the Christian soul of the nation must be unified. Jesus must reign in truth. A Christian patriotism must be supreme. When that time comes, we will then speak, not just an intellectual language, but a spiritual language of mutual understanding.

It is my belief that every church has two duties, namely, a national duty, and a sectarian duty; that it should minister, not only to the souls of its individual members, but to the soul of the nation as well. A church should not confuse the soul of the nation with the souls of its member. It is impossible for America to have a soul that is Methodist, or Baptist, or Presbyterian, or Roman Catholic. It can only have a Christian soul.

When I once traveled in foreign countries, and I could see in the far distance the spire of a church rising high into the air, I always said, I am secure; yonder is civilization. The one thing which held the French together at their most trying moments during the First World War was the thought of the sacred spots over France. Many of those sacred spots were their Christian churches.

During the First World War it was my privilege and opportunity, at one time, to be stationed near the little church where Joan of Arc worshipped. I saw this church and was in it. It is located at Domremy, a short distance back of Verdun. When the French stood at Verdun and said, "They shall not pass," there was the most sacred spot in France only a little way back of them, and that was the spot on which the little church stood in which Joan of Arc worshipped. The Germans did not pass. Verdun did not fall then, and that sacred spot was one of the big reasons. A Christian church is the most valuable asset any community ever has. The Germans "passed" in this war largely because too many Frenchmen had forgotten their sacred spots in France. America, to remain strong, must remember its sacred spots.

Christianity has met every test. For nineteen hundred years it has advanced. Christianity is advancing today in every part of the world, while the so-called old religions of the East are declining.

Hitler, or any other dictator, has no chance to stop the advance of Christianity, because the Christian faith is integral in the souls of the people of Europe. The European way of life and thought, its enthusiasms and reactions all have depended on the Christian outlook. A religion (Pardon me for calling it that) made by a dwarf like Hitler, or any other mere man, cannot stand long against the power and force of Christianity.

Christianity is triumphant, because it has brought peace to many hundreds of millions of souls.

Christianity will be triumphant when the present oppression, persecution, bloodshed, and war is over in Europe; for it is my confident belief that it will again step in and save European civilization.

Everything that I have said may be answered or disputed; but no one can answer a Christian faith and a Christian life. No one can answer Christianity's greatest triumph,—its victory over the grave.

"Yea, though thou lie upon the dust,
When they who helped thee flee in fear,
Die full of hope and manly trust,
Like those who fell in battle here.

"Another hand thy sword shall wield,
Another hand the standard wave,
Till from the trumpet's mouth is pealed
The blast of triumph o'er thy grave."

CHAPTER FORTY-SEVEN

MAN'S INFINITE POSSIBILITIES

Man is distinguished from a brute, in that a brute merely eats, sleeps and dies; while man is endowed with infinite possibilities. It is the realization of these possibilities that characterizes a human being as an individual. When we examine the lower forms of animal life, we find that the species look alike. The fisherman who digs his can of worms will notice nothing that will distinguish one worm from another; they all look alike, except for size. A flock of birds all look very much alike. The most manifest sign of progress is diversity of forms. The higher up we go in the scale of life, the more diverse we find the species. The founders of this great Republic recognized this principle, and left the individual free to realize his infinite possibilities as God intended he should do. They left his conscience free, so that he might fix for himself his relation with God. They left his mind free, so that he might devise as he thought best for himself and his family. They left his speech free, so that he might give to others the results of his thoughts. This has resulted in developing in America, not a nation of automatons, but a nation of individuals, who know how to think and act as God intended man should think and act.

For centuries the American has been in the process of development. Our broad, open country did its part in contributing to this development; it always gave the individual room to expand; it furnished a place where he could remain on the edge of civilization. But we have now come to a place in our history where an effort must be made to keep our individuality. Our country is already settled. The old frontiers are gone. We can no longer move to the edge of civilization. Our cities are becoming crowded. We are getting more and more regulations. All these things tend toward preventing a man from realizing his infinite possibilities and tend to destroy his individuality.

In 1913, in a public speaking contest, as a student in Marshall College, in Huntington, West Virginia, I made the following statement:

"There is a broad highway of progress which America must travel. It is not necessary that she travel exactly in the middle of that highway; but if she is to remain strong and prosperous and healthy she must travel on that highway. She must not get too far to the right or too far to the left. If America goes too far to the right, she will necessarily travel the rough and difficult road of unrestricted individualism, neglecting the poor, the weak and the unfortunate. If America travels too far to the left, she will have to travel in the mire and mud of state socialism, resulting in the destruction of that pioneer spirit which has made America a great nation.

"America must travel that part of the highway of progress which protects the great mass of the people and at the same time leaves open every avenue and incentive for individual effort."

CHAPTER FORTY-EIGHT

WE MUST FIGHT FOR OUR LIBERTY

Our forefathers in the Declaration of Independence said: "We hold these truths to be self evident, that all men are created equal, that they are endowed by their creator with certain unalienable rights, that among these are Life, Liberty and the pursuit of Happiness."

We see that of all the unalienable rights man is endowed with, there were three rights which were uppermost in the minds of the men who signed the Declaration of Independence. These were: The right to life; the right to enjoy liberty; and the right to the pursuit of happiness.

Life, at the best, is always uncertain. We are not always happy. We have had only the right to strive for happiness. But for more than one hundred and fifty years we have actually enjoyed liberty in America. Liberty in this country has become commonplace, so commonplace that we have become accustomed to take it for granted. We have had liberty even though we had to struggle for food, clothing and shelter. We have appreciated the sunshine more than we have our liberty, because at times the sunshine is obscured by the clouds for days, and we are happy when the clouds roll away, and we can feel again the soothing warmth of the sun. Up to this time, we have experienced very few clouds on our sunshine of liberty. Our forefathers fought and bled and died for their liberty. The liberty we enjoy is our heritage.

Powerful enemies of this nation exist in the world today. These enemies have sprung up, not because the people of this country have insulted them, or taken anything away from them, but because they cast an envious eye on the riches Providence has given us, and the riches the energy and the genius of America have produced. The liberty and the future of America are seriously threatened. It is for us today to meet that challenge to our liberty and to our future with the same courage, the same determination and the same vision which our forefathers had when they met their challenge one hundred and sixty-five years ago.

CHAPTER FORTY-NINE

WE CHOOSE OUR OWN DESTINY

No country exists whose history has been marked by the interpositions of God, as much as our own. We are bound to acknowledge an invisible hand in the conduct of our affairs, but the destiny of our country is in our own hands. God will not lead us to greatness against our will, or without our will. We choose our own destiny. This country will be what we make it.

INDEX

INDEX

214